SHAKESPEARE,
Not Stirred

SHAKESPEARE,

Not Stirred

Cocktails for Your Everyday Dramas

Caroline Bicks and Michelle Ephraim

A PERIGEE BOOK

PERIGEE
An imprint of Penguin Random House LLC
375 Hudson Street, New York, New York 10014

SHAKESPEARE, NOT STIRRED

ISBN: 978-0-399-17300-4

This book has been registered with the Library of Congress.

First edition: September 2015

PRINTED IN THE UNITED STATES OF AMERICA

10 9 8 7 6 5 4 3 2 1

Text design by Tiffany Estreicher

CONTENTS

SHAKESPEARE,
Not Stirred

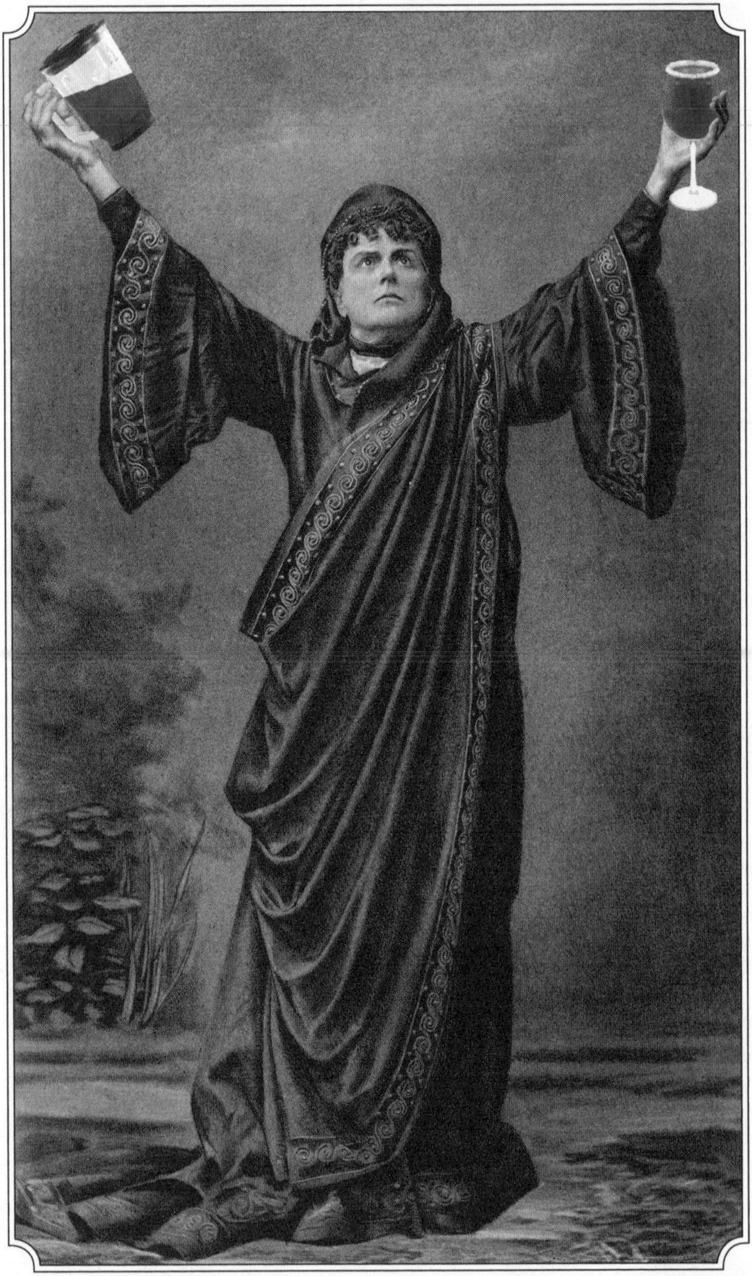

INTRODUCTION

Is This a Daiquiri Which I See Before Me?

If you're wondering what Shakespeare ate and drank when he was living it up in 1599 London, this isn't the book for you. The same goes for all you historical reenactment fans out there. We don't dress up like wenches and go to Renaissance Faires, or serve up foot-long Henry VIII–style turkey legs at our neighborhood block parties.

But we do love Shakespeare. In fact, we've devoted our adult lives to learning as much as we can about his works and his world. We get a geeky thrill out of researching things like sixteenth-century virginity tests and Bible translations. And we never get tired of talking to our students about the themes and moral dilemmas that Shakespeare explores.

We're also close friends who love getting together over a good drink. It's the perfect way to decompress from our everyday dramas—whether it's academic politics, spousal standoffs, or home lice infestations. Frankly, besides Shakespeare, these few hours of high-quality confab are the only thing we *don't* need a break from.

One night, at ye olde Cheesecake Factory, we had an epiphany: the characters we analyzed all day were starting to feel very familiar. And not just because we'd been teaching and writing about them for twenty years. The more we talked, the more we saw ourselves and our problems in *their* comedies, histories, and tragedies. Shakespeare's insights into jealous siblings, shifty coworkers, and aging libidos were smarter than anything we could ever come up with on our own. And a whole lot cheaper than therapy.

Huh, we thought. *This dead guy totally gets us.*

Shakespeare never had to worry about hitting Reply All by mistake, or sending someone's kid to the ER because of a stray peanut trace. But it felt like he was right there with us, sucking down a Factory Peach Bellini and feeling our pain.

We knew right then and there that we'd found our destiny: to write a cocktail book that would pay it forward, Shakespeare-style.

So we got to work, searching every corner of Shakespeare's canon and our liquor cabinets to find the perfect drinks to match our favorite plotlines. We poured, shook, and tasted. Pondered and punned. We were obsessed with our plan—just like the regicidal Macbeth when he hallucinates a murder weapon floating before him. Except our ambitions involved daiquiris, not daggers.

The final product is what you see before you: a book that mixes equal parts booze and Bard to help you through your everyday ups and downs. It's like having him right there in your living room, downing a great drink, and putting your crappy day in perspective.

Each of our cocktails connects Shakespeare's characters to your daily predicaments. And we've paired the drinks with hors d'oeuvres, which we call "Savory Matters." It's our way of repurposing Hamlet's snobby comment about popular entertainment and the commoners who consume it. According to him, *those* people only want "matter savory"—

cheap, spicy jokes and sleazy plotlines. Well, we've got news for you, Hamlet: Shakespeare would have loved Bravo and buffalo wings as much as we do.

Like the editors of the 1623 First Folio, we've organized our Shakespeare into genres—some comical, some tragical, some historical. For example, Girls' Night Out, Drowning Your Sorrows, and Recapturing Your Youth. And if you want to learn more about the plays or the time period, you can raid the Mini-Bards in each chapter for a quick shot of context and commentary. Or not. Unlike Hamlet, we don't judge. The point is, if you want to brush up on your Shakespeare, and maybe learn some things that you didn't know before, fabulous. If you just want to eat and drink, go for it.

Now some of you may be thinking: Booze? Professors? Isn't this why we need to get rid of tenure? But hear us out. Shakespeare wasn't just interested in Fate, Revenge, and Tragic Flaws. His plays are saturated with alcohol-related themes, and it's our job to know about them. Some of these are pretty negative, like (1) Booze and booty don't mix, especially if you're a guy. As the drunken Porter in *Macbeth* says, drinking "provokes the desire but it takes away the performance." Not to mention, (2) Drinking on the job equals career suicide. *Antony and Cleopatra*'s Lepidus learns this lesson the hard way when he blacks out on Pompey's booze cruise and proves he's not Roman Triumvirate material. And, of course, (3) Alcohol makes dysfunctional families even more dysfunctional. Sir Toby Belch, *Twelfth Night*'s "quaffing and drinking" freeloader, upsets his depressed niece by throwing wild parties at her house and calling her a killjoy. And the future King Richard III unleashes a lifetime of sibling hostility by hiring two guys to drown his older brother in a barrel of Malmsey wine.

But drinking in Shakespeare's plays, as in life, doesn't always end in tragedy. Sometimes it's about bringing people together. Building community. Being there for each other through good times and bad. And the timeless power of partying.

We hope that *Shakespeare, Not Stirred* brings you all sorts of pleasure: fun drinks, good food, and the deep satisfaction of knowing that Shakespeare validates all of your feelings—no matter how socially inappropriate they may be. So get out your cocktail shaker and lend him your ears. Has *he* got a story to tell *you*.

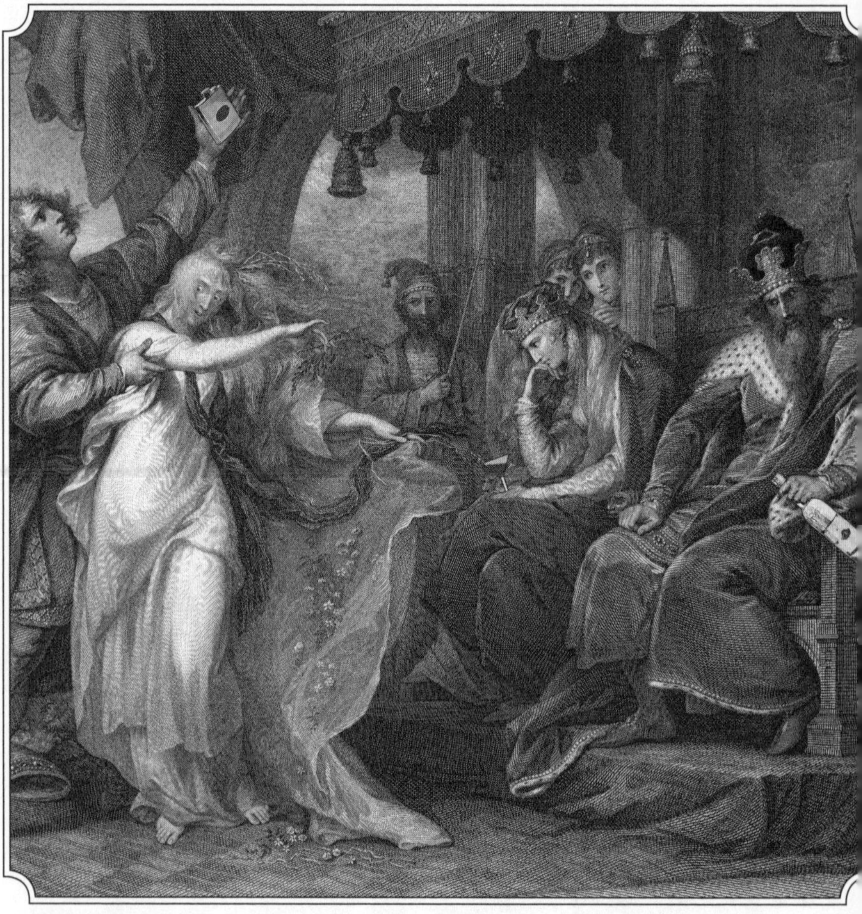

A Little More Than Gin

Dysfunctional Family Gatherings

ou may think you've outgrown your childhood insecurities, but just one family encounter can send you right back to the kids' table. Like when King Lear reignites the sibling rivalry between his adult daughters, Goneril and Regan. After he makes them compete for their inheritance in a "Who Loves Me Most?" contest, they're reduced to their old eyeball-clawing, boyfriend-stealing ways. Meanwhile, over in the rotten state of Denmark, Uncle Claudius rubs salt in Hamlet's Oedipal wounds by calling him "son" at his wedding to Hamlet's mother. The newly fatherless prince mutters: "A little more than kin and less than kind." Loose translation: "You may be sleeping with Mommy, but you are *not* my daddy." Booze is the perfect way to numb the pain of fraught family moments like these. It's not that a stiff drink is the healthiest way to deal with your kin. But it's a lot more enjoyable than hearing about how oversensitive, underachieving, and selfish you are.

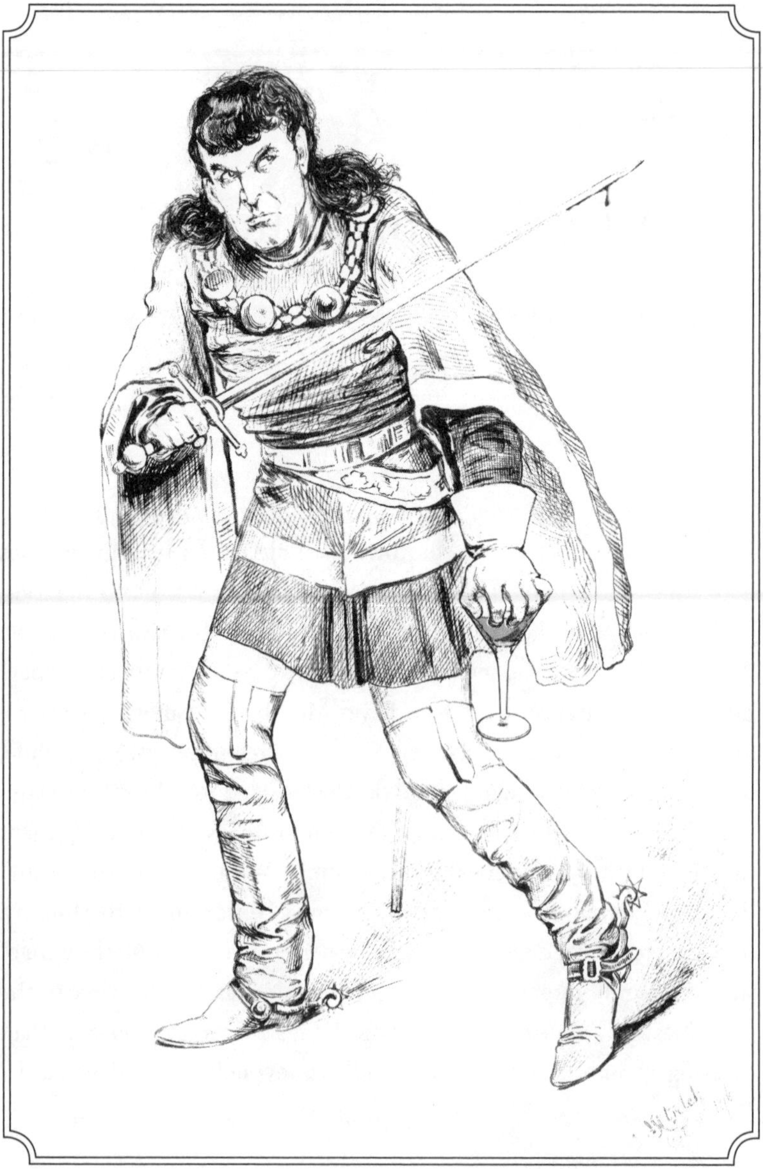

COCKTAILS

RICHARD'S GIMME-LET

Does your family fail to appreciate how special you are? Have you defamed or killed any of them to get what you deserve? Then this drink, mixed in honor of the chronically misunderstood Richard, Duke of Gloucester, is for you. In *Henry VI, Part 3*, Richard scores big for his clan, the Yorks, in the ongoing Wars of the Roses. But at the start of the sequel, *Richard III*, no one cares about any of that. Sure, they all remember his martyr of a dead little brother, Rutland. And everyone's basking in the beams of his newly crowned oldest brother, King Edward. But do they remember one lousy thing *Richard* ever did? *Noooooo*. He's just an uneven-legged hunchback with a withered arm and no girlfriend. What's an undervalued son to do but take down some relatives to get his turn in the Big Chair? Richard spreads a rumor that Edward's a bastard; gets his other brother, George, murdered; and puts a hit out on his little prince nephews just to be safe. And then he gets to be King Richard! Too bad his mother's the only one left to celebrate the big moment. Which she does by crashing his royal procession, announcing he was a monster-baby born "to make the earth my hell," and hitting him with a death curse. At the end of the play, Richard finds himself alone, unloved, and horseless on the Bosworth battlefield, about to be killed by God's gift to England, the future King Henry VII. Face it, Dick, you're a middle child with shoe lifts. This was never going to go your way.

2 ounces gin

½ ounce simple syrup

continued...

1 ounce fresh lime juice

Very thin crosswise slice of habañero pepper

Shake the gin, simple syrup, and lime juice with ice and strain into a martini glass. Drop in a vicious bite of pepper. And in the spirit of Richard's power-grabbing . . . Gimme that drink!

MINI-BARD The historical Richard was actually the youngest York son, but Shakespeare puts him in the middle—which is a great way to play up his status as the overlooked sibling. Other characters get a significant makeover, too. Shakespeare wrote *Richard III* while Elizabeth I was on the throne, so her grandfather Henry VII lands a starring role as the God-anointed hero sent to save England from evil Richard and found the Tudor line. But even if Richard's life and afterlife were full of haters, he has an army of supporters now in the Richard III Society. Founded in 1924, they're a group committed to exposing factual distortions about Richard's life and reign—including his allegedly misshapen body. Congenital disabilities and "unnatural" births were often considered the marks of a damned soul and twisted mind. Sir Thomas More, working under the Tudor regime, knew this when he wrote his 1513 account of Richard's feet-first delivery, hunchback, and villainous behavior. X-ray machines have revealed that a hump was added on to one of Richard's portraits, which lends support to the pro-Richard conspiracy theorists, but the 2012 discovery of his skeleton under a parking lot in Leicester confirms that he had a severely curved spine. After this find, even the Richard III Society publicly acknowledged that "there is a germ of truth behind the Tudor descriptions." Still, as one long-time Society member maintains, "There is no evidence for the hunchback, the withered arm and the limp—they are merely inventions of those trying to blacken Richard's image." *To be continued . . .*

ISABELLA'S VESPERS

In *Measure for Measure*, Isabella is a type A nun-in-training, dedicated to "strict restraint" and fasting, when—*Bam!*—she's forced into a sadistic game of Would You Rather: Would you rather see your brother, Claudio, get executed for illegally fornicating with his girlfriend *or* . . . save his life by having sex with the corrupt autocrat who sentenced him? Isabella, it turns out, would rather not sacrifice her body, her career, and her relationship with God for her "faithless coward" of a brother. Not that anyone could possibly understand that. *Hey, loosen up. It's only your virginity. What's the big deal? You can always get a job waiting tables at the tavern.* Jesus! Does the responsible, "together" sibling *always* have to clean up after the screw-up? Ultimately Claudio gets to keep his life, and Isabella gets to keep her virginity—for the moment—thanks to an undercover duke, a bed-trick, and a pirate head. (There's a reason this is considered a "problem play.") But that doesn't mean she's clear of the whole sordid affair: at the end of the play, everyone expects her to marry the duke, like she's some kind of Edible Arrangements "Thank You" bouquet. Isabella—*girlfriend*—listen to us: Run, don't walk, back to the Sisters of Saint Clare. Then lock yourself in your cell, wait for the evening vespers service, and pray to God that He reincarnates you as an only child. Then treat yourself to one of *these* vespers.

Isabella likes following the rules, so we're sticking to James Bond's classic vesper recipe. But we're adding our own fun garnish of rosary beads and a cross.

10 black tapioca pearls (boba)

3 ounces gin

continued . . .

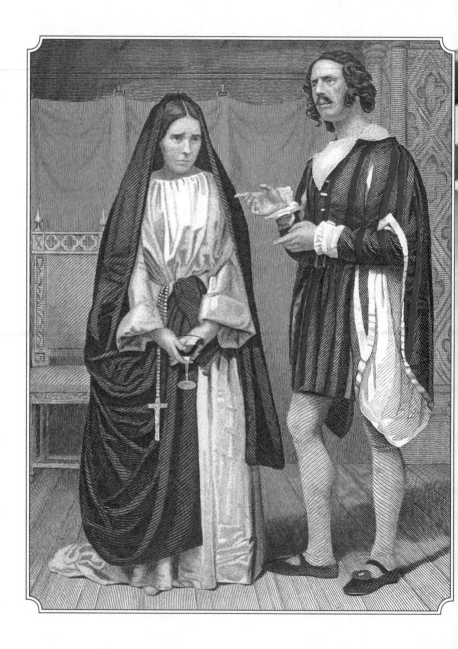

1 ounce vodka

½ ounce Lillet

Lemon peel cut in shape of a cross

Prepare the boba by placing them in boiling water. Cook, covered, for 5 minutes. Drain and cool. Place the cooked pearls in the bottom of a martini glass. Shake (don't stir) the gin, vodka, and Lillet with ice until very cold. Strain into the glass over pearls. Float the lemon peel cross on top.

SHYLOCK'S DUCATS

Every adolescent girl needs someone to rebel against, and in Shakespeare's plays, it's usually Daddy. Okay, so maybe his fathers aren't always super supportive of their little girls' hopes and dreams, but do they deserve to be humiliated by their ungrateful daughters? That's what Shylock, Jessica's tormented Jewish father in *The Merchant of Venice*, wants to know. It's one thing when your daughter sneaks out on a few secret dates—but *eloping*? With a *goy*? And what kind of cruel child takes your wedding ring, along with all your gold and ducats, so she can bankroll her honeymoon to Genoa and her taste for exotic pet monkeys? This drink (made with Goldschläger, a liqueur with actual gold flakes) is for all you heartbroken—and broke—fathers out there. We know you can't afford it, so this one's on us.

Lemon wedge

Edible gold dust

1 ounce Goldschläger schnapps

continued...

Beaten-down dads make frequent appearances in Shakespeare's plays. So it's too bad Shylock's dietary laws prevent him from sharing a consolation drink and some loaded potato skins with all of his equally miserable Christian counterparts. Like Baptista, whose shrewish daughter Kate yells at him for trying to find her a husband, and then embarrasses him by beating up her lute instructor; and Brabantio, whose daughter, Desdemona, breaks his heart when she elopes with Othello, the only non-white guy in all of Venice; and Lord Capulet, who pays for a lavish wedding that Juliet knows she's going to crap out on . . . *by pretending to die.* Even with their bad tempers, racism, and abusive defense mechanisms, Shakespeare's dads can be downright sympathetic at times. They also make us look like great parents by comparison.

3 ounces sparkling cider

1 tablespoon fresh lemon juice

Rim a chilled martini glass with the lemon wedge and dip the rim in gold dust (unless your daughter got to it first). Fill a shaker with ice. Add the Goldschläger, cider, and lemon juice. Shake like you're in Vegas and Daddy needs a new pair of shoes. Strain into the martini glass.

CLAUDIUS'S SEX IN THE BREACH

You knew you weren't the Brady Bunch, but life in your new blended family has been a total pain in the ass. Especially (if you're like Hamlet's stepfather, Claudius) when you have to worry about that moody nephew/stepson of yours and his Big Unmedicated Thoughts, hanging around looking like he wants to kill you. You can't seem to do anything right with that nut-job. First, he thinks you should stop drinking so much, because it's a vulgar Danish custom "more honoured in the breach than the observance" . . . even though you're at your own freaking—hello— *Danish* wedding. Then he's convinced you're breaching some biblical incest command because your new wife also happens to be your sister-in-law. What's next? No more reading on the can? It's time to tune out all the random bitching in your new household and break whatever rules you want. In fact, go ahead and make this Sex in the Breach a double: one for you, and one for your hot "sometime sister, now our queen."

> 2 ounces vodka
> ½ ounce aquavit
> 1½ ounces Orangina
> 1 ounce cranberry juice
> 1 ounce pomegranate juice
> Slice of star fruit

Add the vodka and aquavit (the Danish booze of choice) to a highball glass over ice. Fill with Orangina, cranberry juice, and pomegranate juice and stir. Garnish with star fruit and enjoy the hell out of *this* mixture.

SAVORY MATTERS

GLOUCESTER'S JELLIED EYEBALLS

You know that crazy family who lives down the block? The one with the dad who wanders around the neighborhood naked, yelling at the mail-

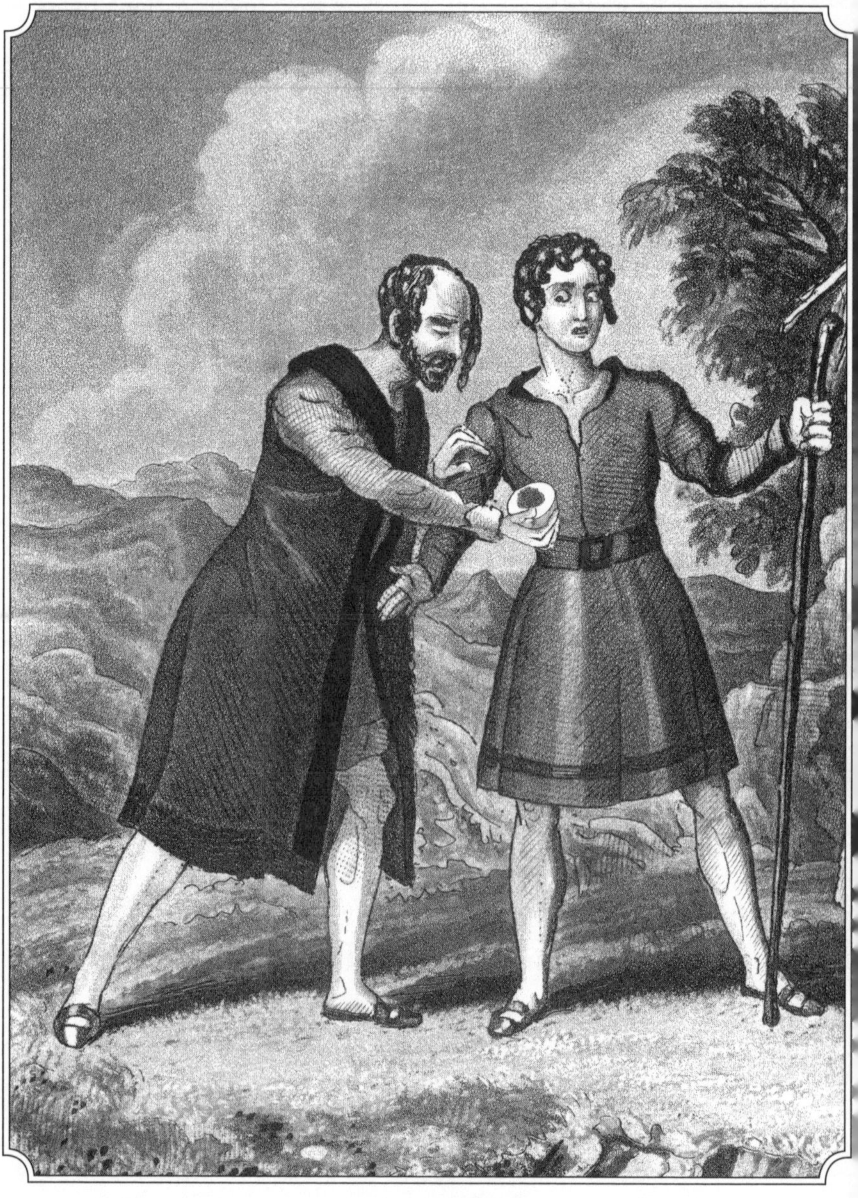

boxes? And the daughters screaming over whose turn it is to give him a sponge bath? Well, take a cue from *King Lear*'s most mangled Good Samaritan, the Earl of Gloucester: Do not—we repeat—*do not* go over there and try to help. If you do, someone might lose an eye. Possibly two. After King Lear makes a mess of his family by disowning his one honest, well-adjusted daughter, Cordelia, and dividing his kingdom up between her devious sisters, Goneril and Regan, he insists they still treat him like he's king. Goneril and Regan shut their doors on him instead, leaving him to wander into a raging storm, where he loses his mind and most of his clothes. That's when Gloucester decides to protect Lear from his daughters' "cruel nails" and "boarish fangs." When Goneril finds out about Gloucester's interference, she decides they should blind him. Regan's on board—in fact, she's practically drooling with excitement as she and her husband, Cornwall, bind Gloucester's "corky arms" to a chair and pluck out one of his eyes. When Cornwall goes for eyeball number two and yells "Out, vile jelly!" it's like a multiple family orgasm. Too bad Gloucester didn't keep his distance from the whole dysfunctional Lear clan. That's what lucky Cordelia got to do. Who *wouldn't* prefer disinheritance to spending one more holiday meal with these sociopaths?

• *40 hors d'oeuvres*

20 small new potatoes, halved crosswise

¼ cup beet juice

1 cup sour cream

¼ teaspoon salt

4 ounces caviar

Boil the potatoes for 15 minutes or until tender. Drain and set aside to cool. Cut a small slice off the rounded bottom of each half so that they can sit flat on a plate. Pour the beet juice into shallow bowl and dab the open face of each potato half in the juice until it takes on a pink hue. Arrange the potato halves on a platter. In another bowl, combine the sour cream with the salt. Spoon a small dollop of sour cream in the middle of each potato. Top the sour cream on each potato with ¼ teaspoon caviar to make the pupils. Continue until all the eyes are staring at you, completely horrified.

Warning: Consuming food that resembles body parts in *King Lear* may evoke negative feelings about your own siblings, favoritism, and the cost of elder care.

⟞⬦⟝

JESSICA'S TOTALLY UN-KOSHER BITES

Shylock's daughter, Jessica, has been cooking up this finger-flip to her dad since she first laid eyes on that dreamy Christian boy, Lorenzo. If all goes well, she'll get the un-kosher kitchen and cutlery of her dreams. This dish mixes shellfish and bacon, and throws in some dairy for good measure. • *12 hors d'oeuvres*

> 6 slices bacon
> ¼ cup maple syrup
> ½ teaspoon red pepper flakes
> 12 jumbo shrimp, peeled, deveined, and tails off
> 3 tablespoons crumbled goat cheese

Preheat the oven to 375°F. Par-cook the bacon in a pan on the stovetop until translucent. Remove from pan, drain, and halve crosswise. Mix the syrup and red pepper flakes together in a small bowl. Brush both

MINI-BARD

When English audiences first heard Jessica gush about ditching her father for Lorenzo to "become a Christian" and his "loving wife," they may have thought: *Great news! The more Christians the merrier!* Then again, they might have questioned the genuineness of her conversion. Jews had long been characterized as untrustworthy and devious. Even murderous. (Medieval stories depicted Jewish men poisoning wells and killing Christian children.) In 1290, Edward I banished all Jews from England, and they weren't legally readmitted until the 1650s. The only official exception to this rule was for converted Jews who were fleeing the Spanish and Portuguese Inquisitions in the fifteenth and sixteenth centuries. This was the case for Rodrigo Lopez, a Portuguese *converso* who fled to England in 1559 and rose to become Elizabeth I's personal physician. Even though he had friends and supporters in the highest places, he eventually was accused of trying to poison the queen. This sensational scandal ended with Lopez's public execution in 1594. Twenty years later, the historian William Camden captured England's enduring distrust of converts when he dramatized Lopez's alleged final moments: the doctor affirmed "that he loved the Queen as well as he loved Jesus Christ: which coming from a man of the Jewish profession moved no small laughter in the standers-by."

---

sides of each shrimp with the syrup mixture, sprinkle with goat cheese, then wrap in bacon. Secure with a toothpick and place on a foil-lined baking sheet. Bake for 15 minutes, or until the bacon is crisp and the shrimp are cooked through.

HAMLET'S "UNWEEDED GARDEN" SPRING ROLLS WITH HONEY DIPPING SAUCE

We really wish Hamlet could have gone to therapy instead of projecting all his issues onto his mother. You just know he blames Gertrude for all of his intimacy problems. Like if it weren't for her "rank and gross" sexual appetite—aka that "unweeded garden" growing in her and Claudius's "nasty sty" of a bed—he'd *definitely* be married to Ophelia. Yeah. *Right.* And they'd be living in the Copenhagen suburbs with their four perfect children, driving over the border to IKEA on the weekends for the $1.99 Swedish meatball breakfast. We can't rewrite Shakespeare, or stop our own kids from blaming us for all their miserable problems, but we can turn Hamlet's crude comment about his mother's "unweeded" hoo-hoo into a healthy finger food. Even if your mother's having incestuous rebound sex with your father's murderer (oops, you weren't supposed to find out about *that* part until the end of act 1), get over it and eat your greens.   • *12 spring rolls*

3 tablespoons sesame oil

2 cloves garlic, peeled and crushed

1 tablespoon minced fresh ginger

½ pound boneless, skinless chicken breast

1 firm mango, peeled and diced

3 carrots, finely grated

½ cup chopped cilantro

1 cup chopped basil

1 cup chopped mint

2 tablespoons seasoned rice vinegar

12 rice paper wrappers

1 cup alfalfa sprouts

6 leaves endive, julienned

3 tablespoons tahini

1½ tablespoons rice vinegar

2 tablespoons soy sauce

1 tablespoon brown sugar

1 teaspoon minced fresh ginger

1 tablespoon coarsely chopped roasted peanuts, for garnish

1 scallion (green part only), chopped, for garnish

In a skillet, heat the sesame oil and sauté the garlic and ginger over medium heat. Add the chicken and cook on high heat until browned and thoroughly cooked. Set aside to cool. Combine the mango, carrots, cilantro, basil, mint, and rice vinegar in a mixing bowl. Shred the cooled chicken and stir with its cooking liquid into this mixture. Prepare the rice paper wrappers, one at a time, by submerging them in a shallow pan of warm water. Lightly pushing down with your fingers, soak the wrapper until translucent and elastic. Lay the wrapper carefully on a flat surface, smooth side down. Place a heaping tablespoon of the chicken mixture at the end of the wrap closest to you. Sprinkle a pinch of alfalfa sprouts and a tablespoon of endive leaves over the filling. Roll halfway up. Fold the sides into the center so they are touching. Roll up to complete.

For the dipping sauce, combine all ingredients except for the garnishes in a small bowl and stir well. Top with peanuts and scallion. Arrange the rolls on plate around the dipping sauce. Call your therapist.

MINI-BARD

Shakespeare's audiences may have felt some déjà vu as they listened to Hamlet rant about King Claudius and Queen Gertrude's "incestuous sheets." Royal incest was front-page news when Queen's Elizabeth's father, Henry VIII, tried to divorce his first wife, Catherine of Aragon, so he could wed Queen Elizabeth's mother, Anne Boleyn. Back in 1503, the pope had granted a special dispensation to Henry so that he could marry Catherine, his brother Arthur's widow, and get around the incest prohibition in Leviticus 20:21, which considered this kind of union "unclean." Then, in 1532, Henry used that very same biblical passage to lobby for the marriage's annulment. His logic? *God was punishing their incestuous marriage by not giving them any boy babies!* Henry's argument didn't fly with the Vatican, so he decided it would be easier to just break with the pope and divorce Catherine himself (see Henry's VIII's Whiskey Slash, page 53). Eventually—after his and his *third* wife's son (yay!) Edward VI took the throne—everyone lived Protestantly Ever After. Sort of. There were, of course, a few unpleasant bumps in the road, including (but not limited to): (1) Protestant Edward's early death, followed by the short reign of his Catholic half-sister, "Bloody Mary," followed by the contentious ascension of her Protestant half-sister, Elizabeth; (2) confusion for everyone over which religion from which monarch you were supposed to be practicing; not to mention (3) which sacrament meant what and why; and (4) panic attacks throughout the land.

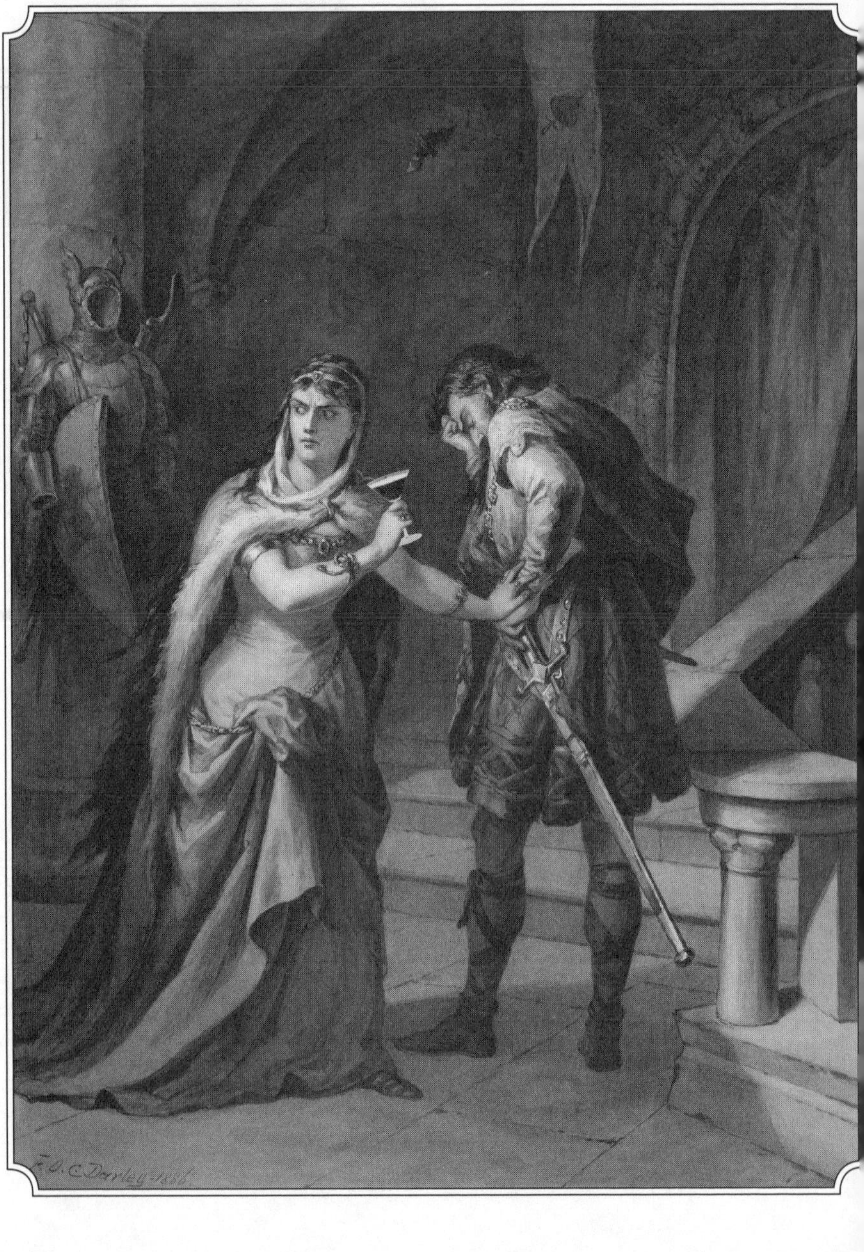
F.O.C. Darley

II

Now Is the Whiskey of Our Discontent

Drinks for the Domestically Distressed

Living in a castle with a stockpile of servants and nurse-nannies may *sound* like a dream come true, especially when you're stuck doing laundry and driving carpool. But Shakespeare's upscale wives had problems, too. Maybe Gertrude didn't have to haul her "gifted" son, Hamlet, around to psychiatric appointments and Russian Math classes, but she did have to deal with all his inappropriate comments about her private life. And how about those husbands? If they aren't accusing you of adultery or shrewishness, they're blaming you for all their career setbacks. At the start of *Richard III*, gloomy Richard's a social outcast who can't snap out of "the winter of our discontent." But, hey, what's *he* complaining about? At least he gets plenty of "me" time. The real tragedy here is that Shakespeare's wives and mothers *never* got left alone. They suffered a lot of grief from a lot of people, and didn't have any girlfriends to back them up and take them out. This group of cocktails and savory matters is for all of you domestically distressed ladies out there looking for a boost of merry fellowship.

LADY MACBETH'S G-SPOT

Calling all ambitious mistresses of the house! Don't end up like Lady Macbeth. At the beginning of *Macbeth*, she strong-arms her husband into murdering his boss, King Duncan, so that they can snag the Scottish throne. Lady M. finally gets her tiara, but it's all so stressful and unpleasant. She ends up wandering around in a nightgown, obsessively washing her hands and sleep talking: "Out, damned spot!" Spilling an anointed king's blood has a way of catching up to you, doesn't it? Lucky for you, the right drink can deliver a satisfying rush of power without staining your furniture—or your soul—with regicidal blood. *This* spot will take you to Cloud Nine, instead of to Hell.

> 2 ounces Scotch whisky
> ½ ounce simple syrup
> ¾ ounce fresh lemon juice
> 10 pomegranate seeds

Shake the first three ingredients with ice and strain into a chilled martini glass. Drop in pomegranate seed "spots" to finish.

KATE'S SHREW-DRIVER

At the end of *The Taming of the Shrew*, Kate's made the bumpy transition from cranky single girl to married lady. She says she's into the obedient wife thing and gives a whole speech telling women to "place your hands below your husband's foot"—but is she for real? After all, Petruchio literally dragged her through the mud and starved her during their honeymoon. We'll never know for sure, but we like to imagine that Kate's happy at least once a week as she's serving these cold, ironic Shrew-drivers up to her married girlfriends at her Wednesday-morning Book Club Brunch. We recommend pairing this sour-lemon version of the classic screwdriver with *Fifty Shades of Grey* or anything by Betty Friedan.

Superfine sugar*
1½ ounces limoncello
1½ ounces lemon-flavored vodka
5 ounces fresh orange juice
4–6 dashes grapefruit or lemon bitters (depending on your
    mood)
Lemon wedge and slice

Rim a highball glass with the lemon wedge and dip the rim in sugar. Fill the glass halfway with ice. Pour in the limoncello, vodka, and orange juice. Stir in the bitters. Garnish with a lemon slice.

---

* Sugar may be replaced with finely crushed Percocet.

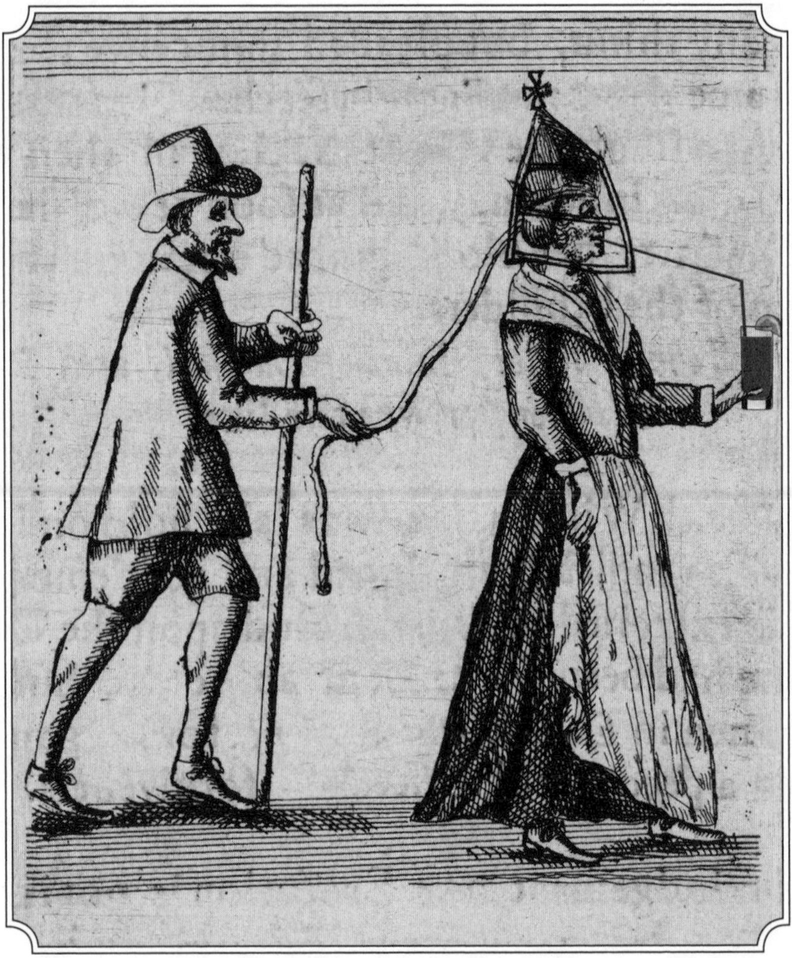

MINI-BARD The Real Housewives franchise didn't exist back in Shakespeare's day, but people sure loved to consume stories about "shrews"—women who yelled at their husbands, or gossiped about their spouses' sex, gambling, and anger-management problems. In other words, women who couldn't keep their big fat traps shut. There were times when a husband had to allow his wife to gossip away—like when she stayed in bed for a month after giving birth, chatting it up with her girlfriends while he took care of the house and paid for the party. But this postpartum gabfest was the exception to the rule. Popular songs and poems about loud, domineering wives usually involved public humiliation, followed by a Stepford-like transformation. If charges of "scolding" were brought against a woman, she might get dunked repeatedly in water and/or muzzled by a scold's bridle, a metal head-cage with a tongue suppressor. The bridle sometimes came with a bonus feature: a leash, for trotting those unruly women out in the streets.

HERMIONE'S MARTYR-INI

Queen Hermione's all smiles when we meet her at the beginning of *The Winter's Tale*. She's blissfully pregnant; her precocious little son, Mamillius, is a charmer; and Polixenes, the best buddy of her husband, Leontes, has just agreed to extend his nine-month visit! But things start tanking fast when Leontes convinces himself that she's a "bed-swerver" who's carrying Polixenes's child. Hermione's forced into a jailhouse birth, Mamillius drops dead, and her newborn's thrown out of the kingdom. Her only option is to fake her own death, hide out for sixteen years, and go through menopause waiting for Leontes to work through his trust issues. Sometimes life calls for hysterical crying. But other times you need to pull a Hermione and quietly suck up your spouse's egotistical behavior in the name of redemption. So the next time he goes off the rails, put on your best stiff smile and make one of these Martyr-inis. Then start planning how you're going to withhold sex from him for the rest of his life.

> 2½ ounces gin
> ½ ounce dry vermouth
> 1 teaspoon olive brine*
> 1 caper berry

Shake the first three ingredients with ice and strain into a martini glass. Garnish with a caper berry.

⎯⎯✧⎯⎯

GERTRUDE'S MILKSHAKE

Little-known fact: baby Hamlet refused to let his mother hand him over to a wet-nurse, so Gertrude had to breast-feed him herself until he was ten. . . . Just kidding! Still, that would explain a lot. Like his obsessive need to control her sex life and suck her dry of whatever fun she's managed to eke out for herself since he left for college (*finally*). When Hamlet returns home and sees the newly widowed Gertrude cavorting with his uncle Claudius, he's repulsed by her inability to stay celibate until the end of time. By his first soliloquy, he's turned her into the poster whore for female weakness: "Frailty, thy name is woman!" You don't

---

* Real tears may be substituted if your guests aren't squeamish about sharing bodily fluids.

need a psych degree to know that *someone* doesn't want to share his mother. We created this sinfully creamy treat in her honor. Go ahead, Gertrude, drink up. This one's all yours—and no one else's. (Unless you want to drink it in bed with your hot new husband, in which case, go for it, lady!)

> 2 ounces vodka
> ½ cup whole milk
> 2 ounces chocolate liqueur
> 3 scoops coffee ice cream
> 1 cup ice

In a blender, mix all ingredients until smooth. Serve in a tall glass with a colorful bendy straw.

SAVORY MATTERS

VOLUMNIA'S BRUISE-CHETTA

It's not easy raising a man of character, especially when you're a single parent like *Coriolanus*'s Volumnia. She's taken a lot of heat from readers over the centuries for getting all excited about her warrior son Coriolanus's multiple war wounds. She waxes poetic imagining the Trojan hero Hector's forehead "when it spit forth blood," and prays that her son will achieve the same glory and the same head injuries. Okay, so she may have pushed Coriolanus into some hyper-violent situations, but she was living the free-range parenting philosophy long before it became hip to let your child walk alone to school and swing from rusty playground equipment. These bruschetta are inspired by Volumnia's commitment to the bruised and bloody school of hard knocks. *Her* kid's got grit. How about yours? • *6 servings*

TOASTED BREAD

1 baguette

Olive oil

1 clove garlic, peeled and halved

Preheat the oven to 375°F. Cut the baguette into ½-inch-thick slices. Brush each side with olive oil and place on a foil-lined baking sheet. Toast for roughly 5 minutes a side. Remove from the oven and immediately rub both sides with the garlic. Serve with either or both of the following toppings:

BLOODY TOMATO TOPPING

1½ cups diced ripe tomatoes

15 large basil leaves, chopped

2 cloves garlic, minced

1 tablespoon balsamic vinegar

½ teaspoon kosher salt

Mix all ingredients together in a bowl and let sit for at least 30 minutes. Put a heaping spoonful on toasted bread and serve.

BRUISED BLUEBERRY TOPPING

1 cup blueberries

2 teaspoons balsamic vinegar

½ cup (4 ounces) goat cheese

¼ cup chopped mint leaves

Sea salt (black, if you can find it)

Chop up the blueberries and macerate in the vinegar for 15 minutes. Spread a generous amount of goat cheese on each piece of toasted bread. Mound bruised blueberries on top. Sprinkle with mint and sea salt.

CLEOPATRA'S FLINGS IN A BLANKET

Call Cleopatra what you will—floozy, home wrecker, destroyer of the Roman Triumvirate (blah, blah, blah, she's heard it all). But could *you* balance a kingdom, four kids, a staff of eunuch slaves, and a constant stream of demanding high-level executive lovers? Cleopatra had a serious day job ruling Egypt from 50 to 31 BCE, but that didn't stop her from making time for sexy fun at night. She was always inventing creative ways to keep her baby daddies, Julius Caesar and Mark Antony, in full-on worship mode. This dish is a tribute to one of her most famous tricks: sneaking into Caesar's apartment wrapped in a blanket. It's an aphrodisiac gently massaged with cream sauce, gripped tightly by a piece of meat, and then plunged through with a sword. (Um, is it getting hot in here?) • *24 hors d'oeuvres*

1 pound thinly sliced steak

1 cup Worcestershire sauce

2 tablespoons crème fraîche

1 tablespoon Dijon mustard

continued...

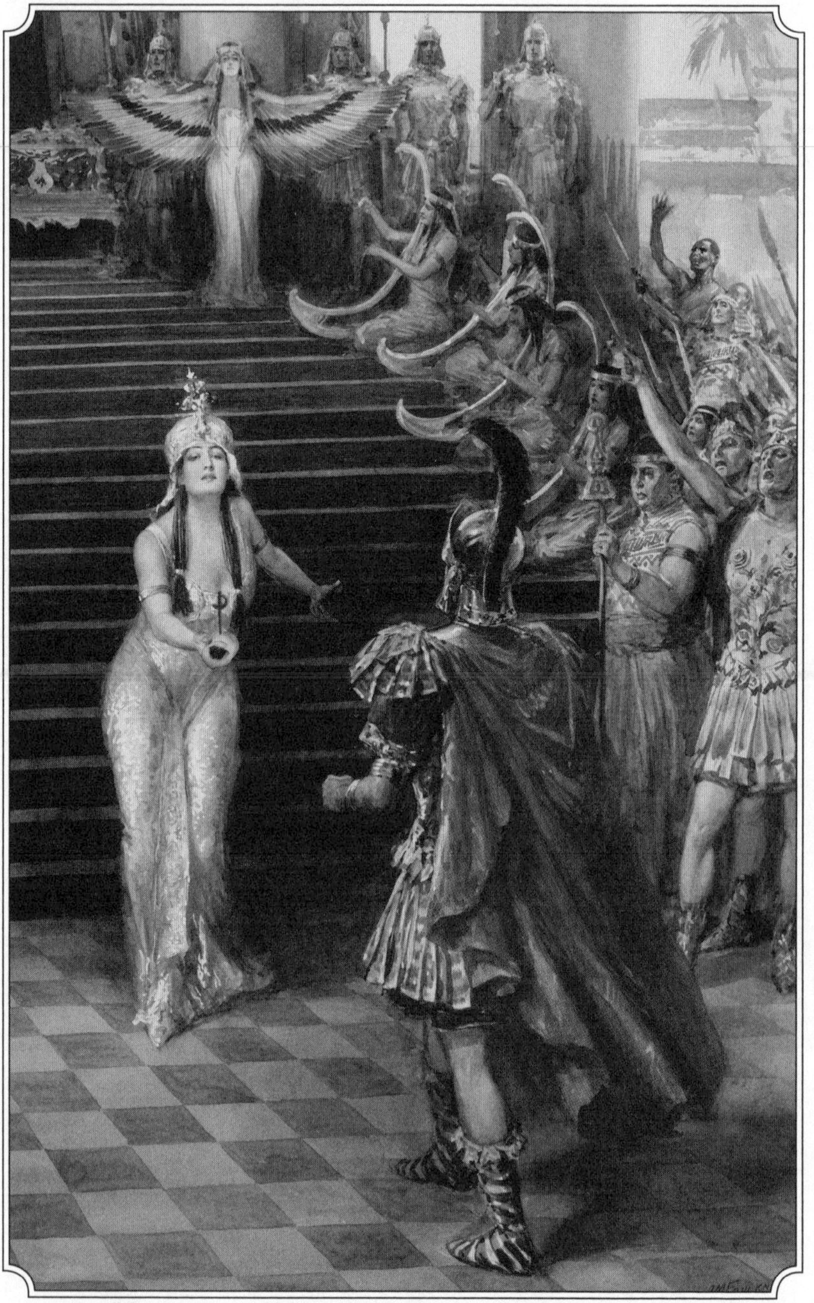

MINI-BARD Shakespeare stuck closely to his historical sources when he wrote *Antony and Cleopatra*—primarily Sir Thomas North's 1579 translation of Plutarch's *Lives of the Ancient Grecians and Romans*. That's where he would have read about Cleopatra's list of powerful Roman admirers. In Shakespeare's play, Cleopatra reminisces about her days as Julius Caesar's lover, when she was "a morsel for a monarch," and how Pompey the Great "would stand and make his eyes grow" while staring at her gorgeous face. Shakespeare does depart from his sources in a few interesting ways, though. He makes Antony's marriage to Octavia short and child-free, while playing up Cleo's iron-mama image: the asp that kills her sucks from her breast instead of her arm. *Hello, La Leche League? I think you've found your new chapter president for the Eastern region.*

1 teaspoon fresh lemon juice
1 teaspoon apple cider vinegar
½ teaspoon crushed garlic
Salt and pepper
24 smoked oysters
Plastic sword toothpicks

Marinate the beef slices in the Worcestershire sauce in the refrigerator for 4 to 6 hours. Thoroughly mix the crème fraîche, mustard, lemon juice, vinegar, and garlic. Season with salt and pepper, to taste. Panfry the steak until medium-rare. Cut the steak slices into ½-inch-wide, 3-inch-long strips. To assemble each Fling, slather cream sauce on a steak strip. Then place an oyster at the end of the strip and roll up. Plunge a sword toothpick through each Fling.

IMOGEN'S GUACA-MOLE

Shakespeare put his wife characters through a lot of Extreme Challenges—like being buried alive and walking hundreds of miles to have sex. In fact, the longer he wrote, the more bizarre those trials became. Imogen, from his late play *Cymbeline*, endures an especially cruel set of hardships. First she's banished by her father for marrying her true love, Posthumus. Then Posthumus accepts a wager from an evil Italian who claims he can seduce Imogen. He can't, but he convinces Posthumus that he's done the deed by describing the mole on his wife's naked breast—a mark "right proud / Of that most delicate lodging." Disowned by her faithless spouse, Imogen has to live in the forest dressed like a boy, drink death-sleep potion, and wake up next to a headless corpse, before reuniting with that gem of a husband. You know what, Imogen? Is this really the person you want to be spending your precious time with? Why not mix up a bowl of this guac, reclaim your mole, and invite your new girlfriends from the SlanderedWomyn chat room over to watch *Thelma & Louise* instead?   • *4 cups*

    4 ripe avocados
    Juice of 1 lemon
    ½ teaspoon garlic powder
    1 teaspoon salt
    6–8 dashes Tabasco sauce
    ½ black olive

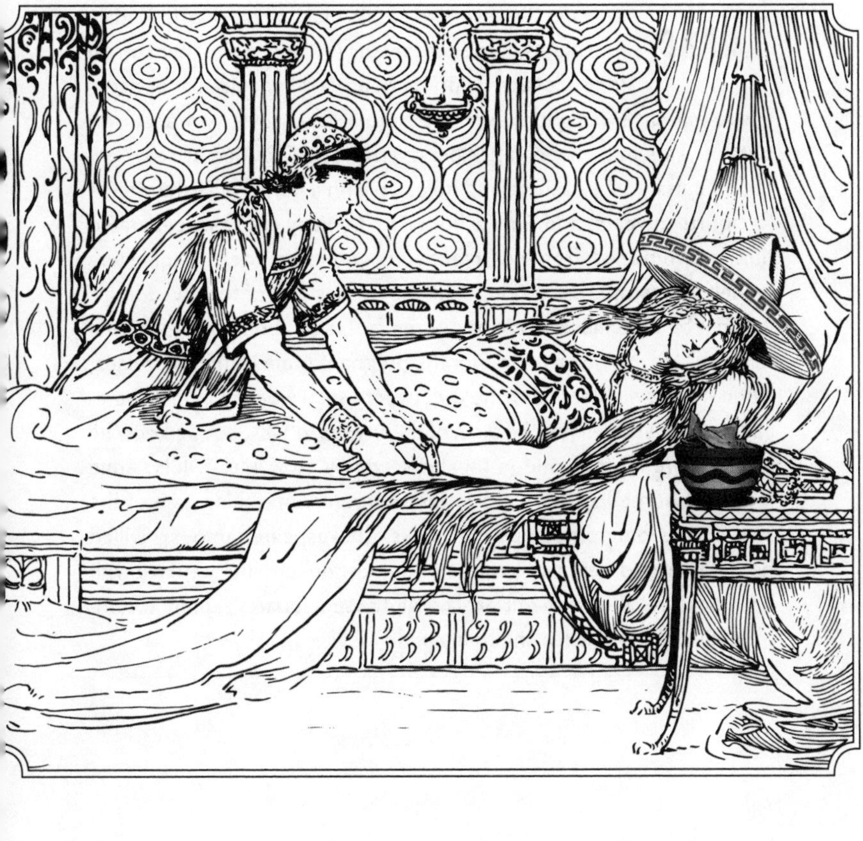

Scoop out the avocado into a bowl and mash with a fork. Mix in the lemon juice, garlic powder, salt, and Tabasco. Adjust the seasoning to suit your preference. Place the olive "mole" on top and serve.

MINI-BARD

Why did Shakespeare put so many of his married ladies into states of pseudo-death? And then send them off on long, cloistered "praycations" with no juice bar or deep-tissue massage in sight? Hermione's stuck faking her own death for sixteen years in a chapel; after being erroneously buried at sea, *Pericles*'s Thaisa washes ashore and holes up with a bunch of vestal virgins for fourteen years; and Emilia from *The Comedy of Errors*, separated during a shipwreck from her infant sons and left for dead, sequesters herself in a temple for so long that she misses one of their weddings. Could it be that Shakespeare had some fantasies about long-term wife removal? He married a three-months-pregnant Anne Hathaway in 1582, when he was eighteen and she was twenty-six. Evidence of his where-abouts gets spotty after the birth of their twins in 1585, but we know he was a figure on the London theater scene by 1592. Meanwhile, Anne stayed at home in boring old Stratford-upon-Avon taking care of the kids and fending off plague outbreaks. Shakespeare famously willed her his "second best bed" in one of the few documents we have with his signature. Which might explain all those subpar sleeping accommodations he keeps leaving to his fictional wives.

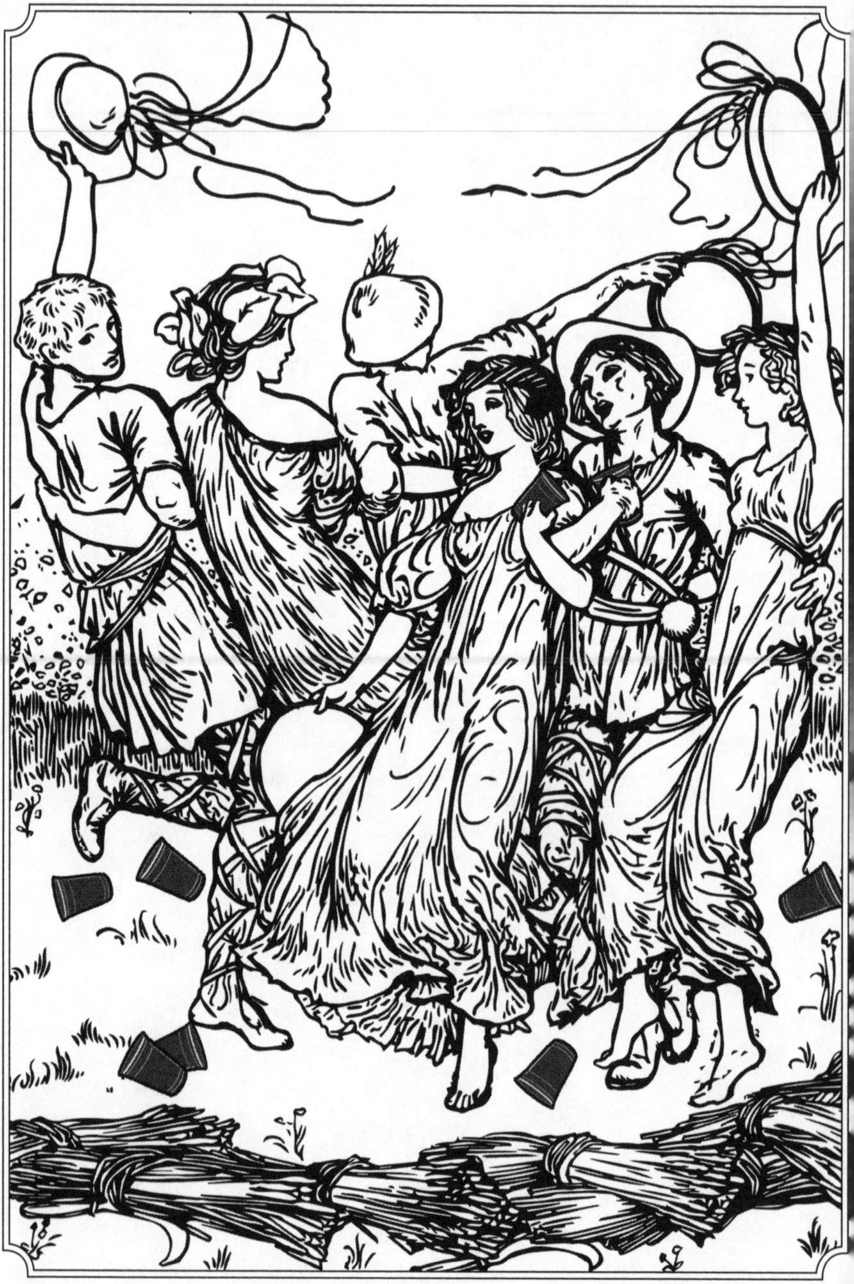

III

Jäger Cannot Wither Her

Recapturing Your Youth

Shakespeare loved to write about young people. After all, he knew hormonal hijinks were a guaranteed crowd-pleaser. Who doesn't enjoy taking a trip down memory lane (assuming you still have one), reminiscing about endless sex drives, poor judgment calls, and the self-destructive hilarity that ensues? It's not that anyone actually wants to relive their cystic acne and failed contraceptive devices, but wouldn't it be great to harness Cleopatra's youthful attitude? She's no teenager, but she sure acts like one in *Antony and Cleopatra*. Especially when it comes to her late-night partying, prom queen theatrics, and "immortal longings." Enobarbus puts it best when he describes her refusal to slump toward elastic waistbands and early-bird specials: "Age cannot wither her, nor custom stale / Her infinite variety." Maybe it's time to break out of your safe routines and make like an unpredictable teen. These drinks and munchies are your first step toward recapturing that fresh adolescent spirit.

THE FOREST FLIER

Ah, the forest: Shakespeare's favorite place to send young people looking to fly from authority. Hermia and Lysander, the forbidden lovers in *A Midsummer Night's Dream*, jump Athens' walls to escape together into the woods. And that wacky *As You Like It* trio of Rosalind, Celia, and their clown friend defy the iron-fisted Duke Frederick by running away to the Forest of Arden. Whatever their reasons for going, no one ever comes back from the "forests wild" without *some* crazy story to tell (or a wicked hangover and a vague memory of a catfight and a threesome gone bad). Even if you never snuck away from home to romp in the woods, you probably lied to your parents about a late-night study group so you could meet up with friends in the park to swig Jägermeister. We've replaced that heavy, calorie-laden drink with its lighter cousin, sambuca, so you can get a hit of your rebellious, Jäger-pounding days without wasting all your Weight Watchers points. And if you really want to break some rules, light your Flier with a match and watch it go up in flames. *Whoaaaaa.*

> ½ ounce 151 proof Spirytus (or grain-neutral
>   spirit of equal or greater proof)
> ½ ounce sambuca

Shake all ingredients with ice. Strain into a mini Solo cup. Or, if setting on fire, a shot glass.

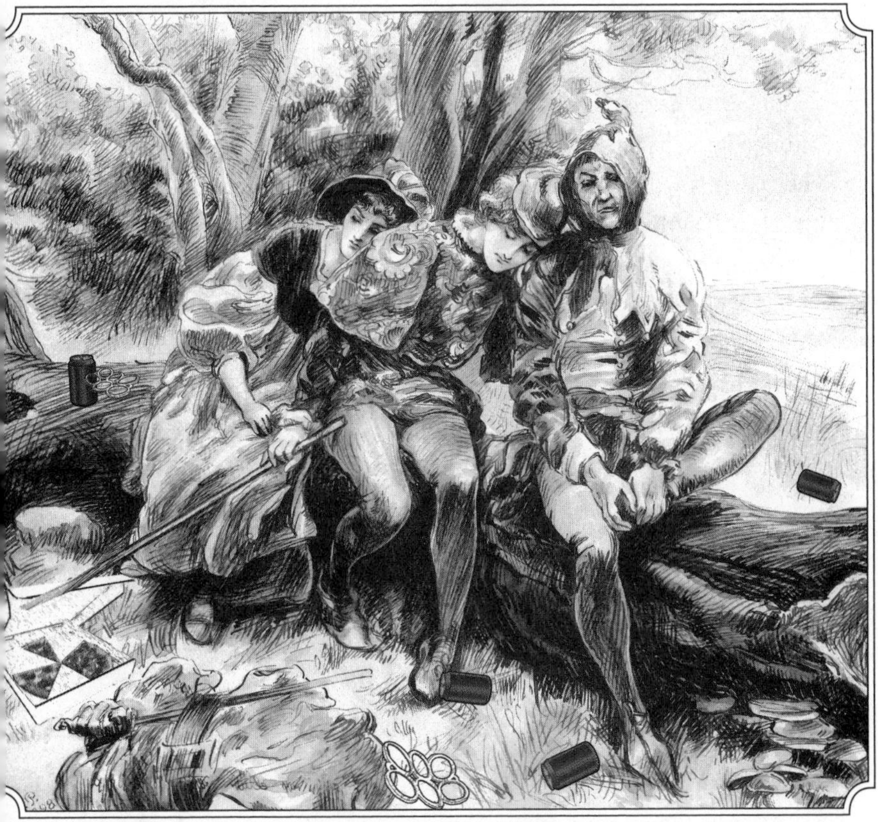

JULIET'S EMOJI-TO

When you're a teenager living in a Shakespeare play, you can't just spew your emotions out on social media. Especially if you're a young lady from a noble family, like thirteen-year-old Juliet Capulet. She has to cram all of her larger-than-life passions into tidy metaphors and controlled iambic pentameter lines. So when she's freaking out about how her parents will never ever *ever* let her be with her One True Love because he's a Montague and because they just don't understand *anything* and don't care about how *miserable* she is because they don't even know what True Love *is* . . . it comes out as: "What's in a name? That which we call a rose / By any other word would smell as sweet." If only Juliet could have let loose in Emoji. And then shared it all on Twitter. And Instagram. And Snapchat. And Tumblr.

> 2 tablespoons chopped mint leaves
> 1½ tablespoons sugar
> 5 fresh cherries, pitted
> ½ lime, cut into four pieces
> 2 ounces white rum
> Splash of seltzer
> Lime wedge

Muddle the mint, sugar, and cherries at the bottom of a heavy glass (if possible, one with a smiley face decoration). Add the lime pieces and muddle again. Fill the glass with ice and pour in the rum. Stir gently. Add a splash of seltzer, squeeze in juice from the lime wedge, and drop it on top to finish.

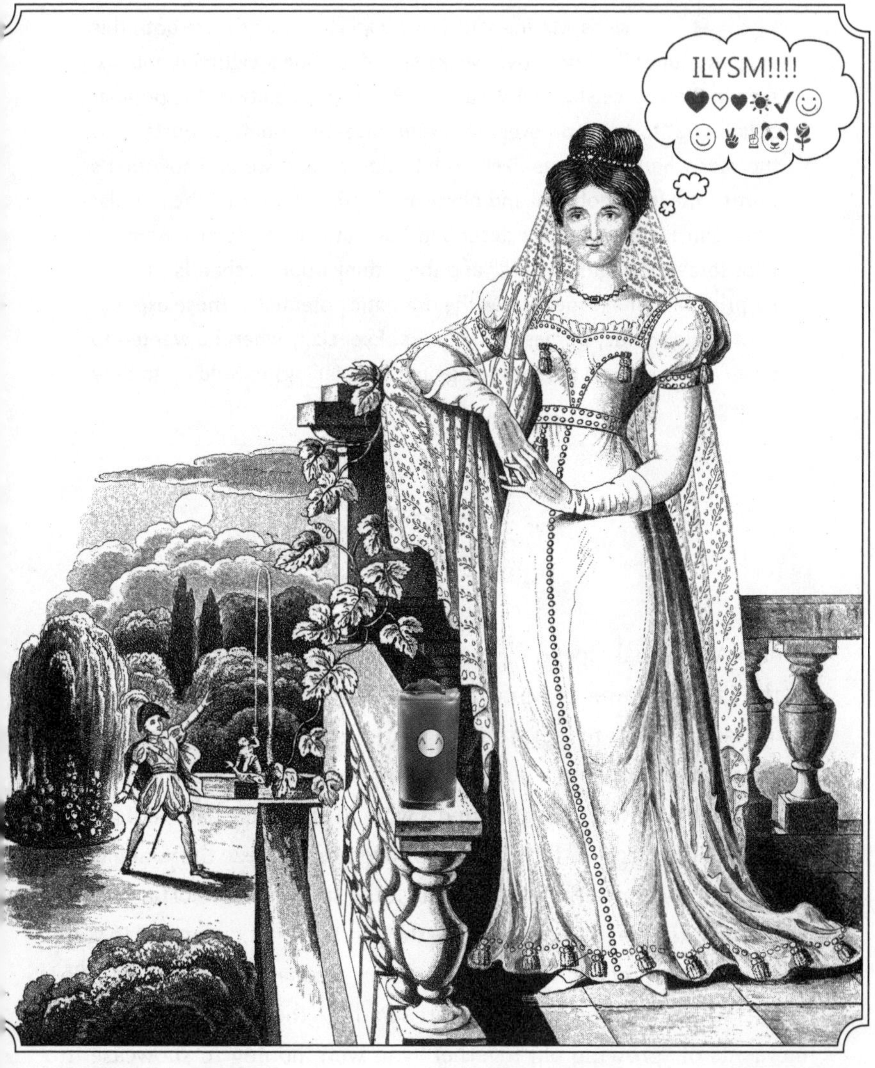
ILYSM!!!!

MINI-BARD Shakespeare never tells us exactly how old his characters are—unless they're fourteen-year-old girls. *Pericles*'s Marina and *The Tempest*'s Miranda are both this age, and Juliet is almost two weeks shy of it. (She's eighteen and sixteen in the source stories.) What gives? One possibility is that popular belief—not to mention everyday experience—pinpointed fourteen as the year when a girl was likely to hit puberty, and we all know that's prime time for emotional and physical . . . growth. In 1615, the popular physician Helkiah Crooke described how, at age fourteen, "womens paps [breasts] begin to swell" and they "think upon husbands." It's no surprise that Shakespeare saw the dramatic potential in these expanding female minds, bodies, and libidos. Especially when he wanted to create stories about parents struggling (and failing) to hold on to their little girls.

THE YOUNG MAN-HATTAN

Spoiler Alert: Shakespeare's 154 sonnets aren't the Most Moving Tribute to the Eternal Power of Mutual Love Ever Written. They're about one man's failed efforts to recapture his youth. The speaker spends the first 126 sonnets addressing a young man whom he loves. He hopes to (1) convince this "lovely youth" to find a woman and make babies that will reproduce his gorgeous face; and (2) cryogenically freeze the young man in iambic time, preserving him through the speaker's immortal poetry. Either way, the speaker wants to use the youth's genetic material to stop his *own* aging process: "My glass shall not persuade me I am old / So long as youth and thou are of one date." Perhaps these weren't the loving moments of "growing old together" you were hoping to showcase in your wedding readings. Especially the one where the young man takes a turn with a woman now known as the Dark Lady, a mysterious brunette who's the subject of the last twenty-eight sonnets. The jealous speaker makes peace with this betrayal by deciding that when the Dark Lady sleeps with his friend, it's kind of like she's sleeping with *him*. Because "my friend and I are one." Huh. *Or* like *he's* sleeping with the young man, too. By association. Or maybe he can just stay and watch, and write a poem about it. And maybe take some pictures? Our fresh twist on the classic Manhattan lets you, like Shakespeare's speaker, go on a quest for everlasting youth—without having to worry about restraining orders.

 MINI-BARD Sonnet sequences, first perfected by the fourteenth-century Italian poet Petrarch, were hugely popular in Shakespeare's day. Some writers used them to impress their friends, gain patrons, or (as many critics think about Shakespeare's poem-writing days) remain productive during times of plague-related theater closings. Sonnet sequences usually focus on three main themes: desire, writing, and writing about desire. In Sir Philip Sidney's *Astrophel and Stella*, the speaker spends 108 sonnets and eleven songs pining for an elusive woman. Edmund Spenser's *Amoretti* tells a more successful love story of wooing and winning his wife. And Richard Barnfield wrote sonnets about male-male love. But Shakespeare is unique in penning a collection of sonnets about homoerotic desire, sex addiction, *and* a mistress whose breath "reeks." The fact that he puns on the name Will (slang for both male and female genitalia) in the sonnets written to the Dark Lady has led many to assume Shakespeare and the speaker are one and the same. We'll never know for sure, but we can recognize high-quality smut-punning when we see it: "So thou, being rich in Will, add to thy Will / One will of mine to make thy large Will more" (Sonnet 135). Put *that* in a Hallmark card and smoke it.

2 ounces WhipperSnapper Oregon Whiskey
(or whiskey of your choice)
1 ounce amaro
2 dashes Angostura bitters
Maraschino cherry

Shake the whiskey and amaro together with ice. Strain into a martini glass. Add the bitters. Drop in a cherry to finish.

~❧~

VIOLA'S SALTY DOG

In *Twelfth Night*, Viola washes up on the salty shores of Illyria after a shipwreck. Then she decides to dress like a boy and take a job as Duke Orsino's servant. Next thing you know, she has a big ol' panting-like-a-dog crush on him! To make matters worse, the duke orders her to deliver his love messages to Countess Olivia *and* listen to the cheesy playlists that remind him of her. Viola feels like a "poor monster" with a massive identity crisis, but—hey—who hasn't been there? Remember freshman year, when you fell in love with your dorm RA—the one who asked you to feed her cat whenever she slept at her boyfriend's? She didn't know your last name, but you knew her favorite Joni Mitchell song and her sun sign. It was all so devastating and exciting and horrible and . . . freaking *amazing*! This Salty Dog brings back those thrilling, masochistic shipwrecks of your youth. Except now you get to drink the salt without drowning.

Lime wedge
5 thyme sprigs

Juice of ½ lime

2 tablespoons maple syrup

2 ounces ruby-red grapefruit juice

2 ounces gin

Fine sea salt

Rim a lowball glass with the lime wedge and dip the rim in sea salt. Muddle 3 thyme sprigs, the lime juice, and the maple syrup in the bottom of the glass. Fill the glass with ice and pour in the grapefruit juice and gin. Stir gently and garnish with the remaining thyme sprigs.

⚬ SAVORY MATTERS ⚬

LUCIO'S CRABS CAKES

When you're young, you feel invincible. *Nothing bad could ever happen to me*, you think. So what if you got a little burning itch after that random hookup? It's nothing a little mercury won't clear up. But, as Lucio in *Measure for Measure* learns, this "foppery of freedom" can't last forever. After he boasts about all the diseases he's purchased at the local brothel, the pregnant prostitute Kate Keepdown claims he's her baby daddy, and Lucio's left staring down the barrel of lifetime child support. This zesty twist on a classic infestation takes you back to those carefree days when you thought an embarrassing exchange with a pharmacist was the worst of your problems.   • *16 hors d'oeuvres*

1 pound lump crabmeat

¼ cup mayonnaise

½ cup finely chopped red bell pepper

3 scallions (green parts only), chopped

1½ teaspoons Old Bay Seasoning

3 tablespoons panko bread crumbs

Salt and pepper

1 egg

½ cup all-purpose flour

¼ cup vegetable oil

MINI-BARD If you were an unmarried English maid or man, sex could be a high-risk proposition. Forget catching crabs—you might get a case of the French pox (aka syphilis). People feared that young Englishmen would return with this souvenir after spending their Renaissance equivalent of a gap year in Europe, or serving as soldiers abroad. And then there was the danger of out-of-wedlock births. If a woman named the father of her child, he'd be obligated to take responsibility, but in too many cases she was left to fend for herself. A number of these pregnancies were the result of sexual advances (violent and otherwise) made on the many single women working and living away from home. Other unplanned pregnancies came from a lack of pre-wedding impulse control. Roughly 25 percent of brides-to-be (including Shakespeare's own intended, Anne Hathaway) were expecting before they got to the altar, which wasn't a problem as long as the wedding went as planned (and you didn't live in a parish that prosecuted premarital fornication). But if a nuptial contract was broken before the wedding day, a pregnant bride was demoted to bastard bearer. And if the contract had been common knowledge, then her ex got his own share of public shaming—*and* the tab.

¼ cup mayonnaise

1 teaspoon sriracha

Mix together the crabmeat, mayonnaise, bell pepper, onions, seasoning, and bread crumbs. Season with salt and pepper, to taste. Fold in the egg. Form the crab mixture into 1-inch-diameter patties. Coat each patty in flour. Heat the oil over medium heat. Place the patties in the pan and cook for 3 minutes on each side. Remove and drain on a paper towel. Prepare the topping by mixing together mayonnaise and sriracha. Place a small dab of topping on each cake and serve immediately.

PUCK'S MAGIC 'SHROOMS

In *A Midsummer Night's Dream*, Puck, a "shrewd and knavish sprite," puts magic "love juice" in Lysander's and Demetrius's eyes, which causes all kinds of psychedelic girlfriend swapping. He'd probably love to bake up some magic 'shrooms and mess with *your* head, too. But unlike the ones you tried back in your experimental years, these fungilicious treats won't impair your ability to operate heavy machinery or look people in the eye the next day.   • *50 hors d'oeuvres*

6 tablespoons olive oil

3 medium golden beets, peeled and diced

50 button mushrooms, washed and stems removed

Salt and pepper

1 cup (8 ounces) goat cheese, room temperature

2 tablespoons finely chopped fresh rosemary or thyme

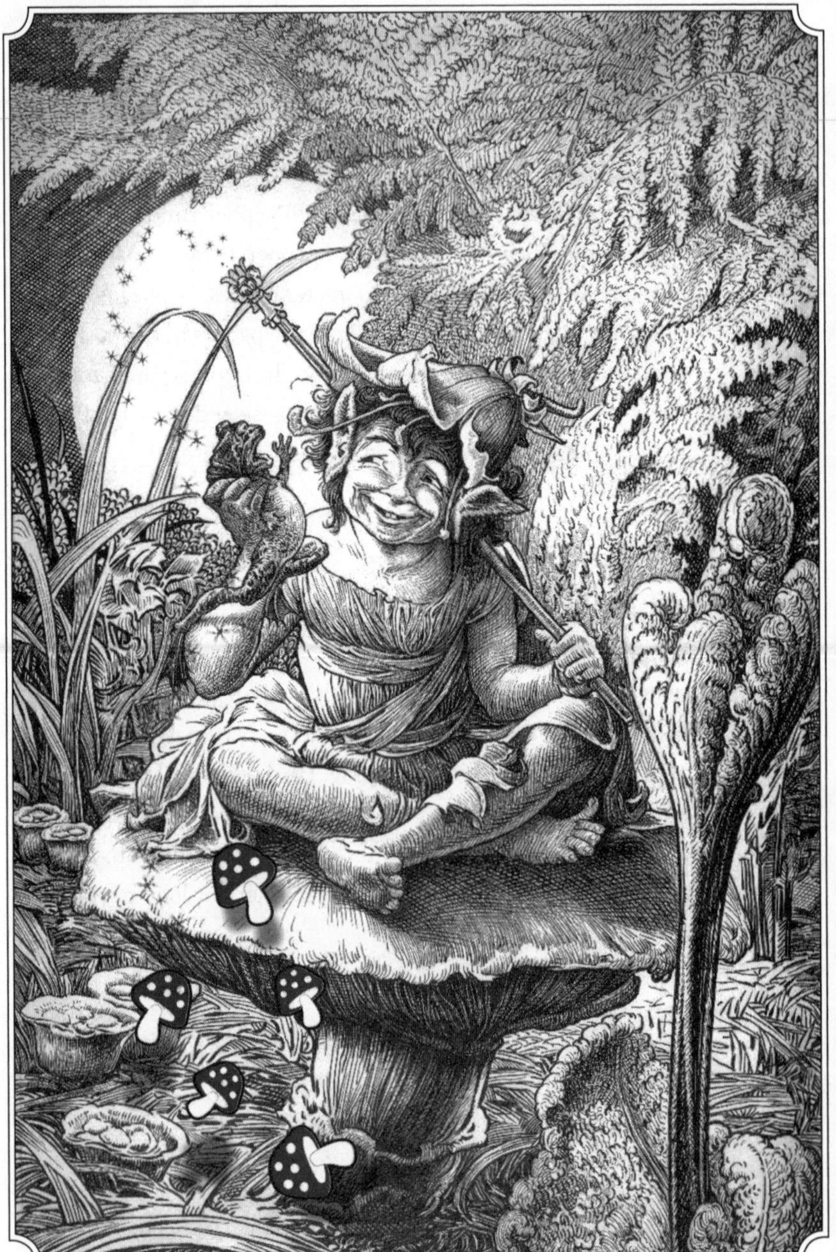

Preheat the oven to 375°F. In a large skillet, heat 4 tablespoons olive oil. Panfry the beets on medium-high heat until they turn light brown and crispy (13–15 minutes). Set aside. In a large bowl, lightly coat the mushrooms with the remaining 2 tablespoons olive oil and salt and pepper, to taste. Mix well. Arrange the mushrooms rounded side down on a baking sheet and bake for 25 minutes (the middles will fill with liquid). Flip the mushrooms and bake for another 20 minutes. While they are cooking, prepare the filling by blending the goat cheese and herbs in a small bowl. Arrange the cooked mushrooms on a platter. Fill liberally with the cheese mixture and top with the beets. Eat the 'shrooms. Close your eyes. Love everyone.

HERO'S PITY PÂTÉ

What would you do if your first and only true love dumped you with no warning? Would you pretend to be dead until he decides he likes you again? If you answered "Yes! Totally!" then *Much Ado About Nothing*'s pitifully patient Hero is your Shakespearean double. Young lovebirds Claudio and Hero are crazy about each other—that is, until John the Bastard tricks Claudio into thinking Hero's cheating on him. What should have been the happiest day of her life is ruined when Claudio calls her a "rotten orange" and breaks up with her in front of all their wedding guests. Not unlike her tragic doppelgänger, Juliet, Hero takes a friar's advice and plays dead while things work themselves out. (Fingers crossed!) It's a lot like that 1988 spring break you wasted waiting by the phone for your ex-boyfriend to call while your roommates were on that awesome booze cruise in Fort Lauderdale. If, after all these years, you're even remotely tempted to erect a Facebook "In Memoriam" page for yourself to see if he posts something nice . . . STOP. You'll just end up feeling sorry for yourself. Leave that pathetic girl behind and get yourself to *this* Pity Pâté instead. • *2 cups*

7 ounces firm tofu, drained
1 cup raw almonds
1 medium carrot, peeled and parboiled
1 tablespoon Worcestershire sauce
1 scallion (white part only), chopped
1 teaspoon salt
1 clove garlic, minced
¼ teaspoon ground cumin
¼ teaspoon ground coriander
1½ teaspoons olive oil
¼ teaspoon minced fresh ginger
½ cup chopped parsley
1½ tablespoons fresh lemon juice
1 tablespoon orange juice (fresh, not rotten, please)
Chopped almonds, for garnish

Combine all ingredients except for the garnish in a food processor and blend until almost smooth. Place in a small bowl lined with plastic wrap. Refrigerate for 2 hours. Turn the bowl over onto a platter and remove the plastic wrap to create a molded pâté. Top with chopped almonds. Serve with crackers and sighs . . . of relief that you're not making a total fool of yourself right now.

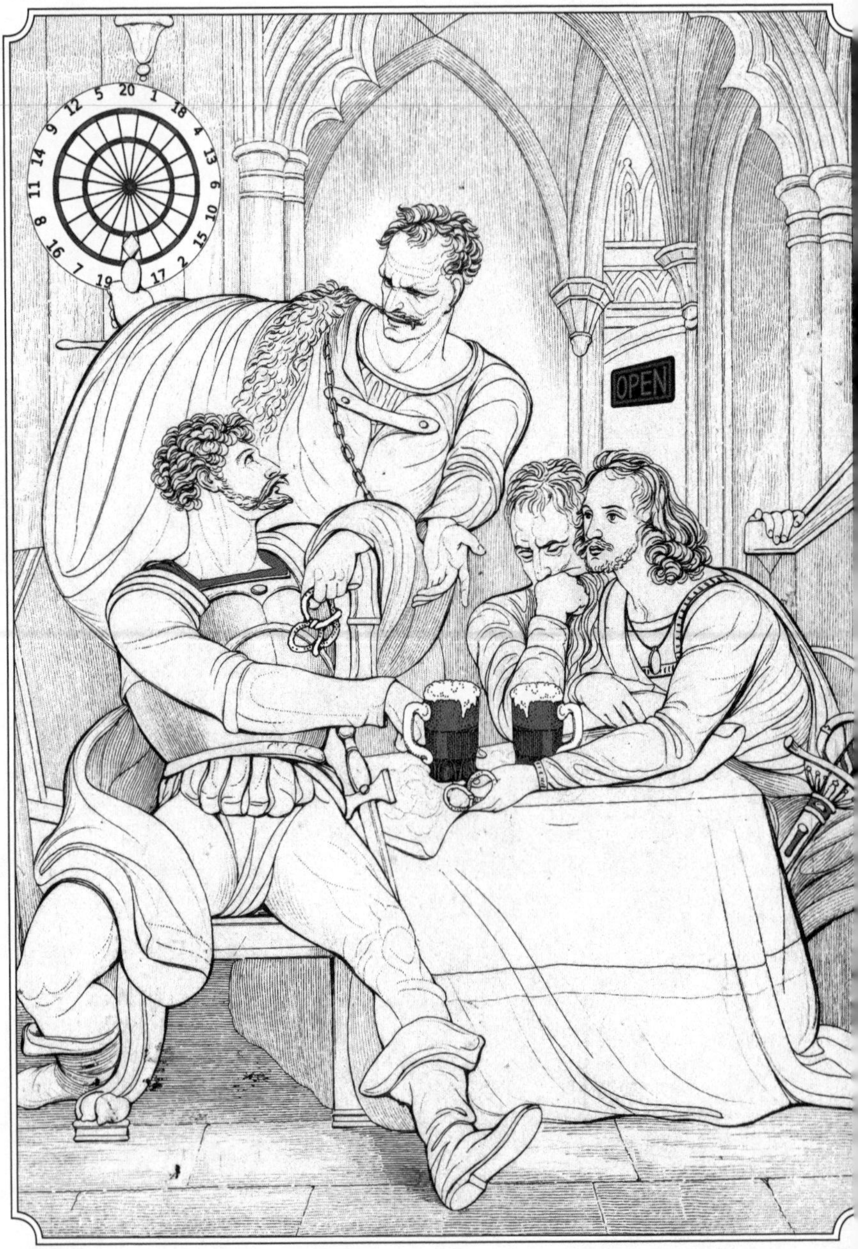
20 1 18 4 13 6 10 15 2 17 19 7 16 8 11 14 9 12 5
OPEN

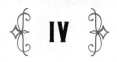

Screw Your Courage to the Swigging Place

Man Time

When Macbeth has second thoughts about killing King Duncan, his wife tells him to man up and "screw your courage to the sticking-place." It works. But a Real Man's supposed to know how to screw everything on his own—which can put a lot of pressure on a guy. Sure, it's nice being able to snap your fingers and get rid of your country's religion or your whorish fifth wife. And of course it's a great perk to have magical powers and use them against anyone who messes with your plans for colonial and domestic domination. But a Man's life isn't all celebrity executions and hot procreative sex. Shakespeare understood the stresses of succeeding at work, keeping the wife and kids in line, *and* finding time to demolish your belly fat. These drinks are the perfect way to leave behind a day filled with hostile wombs and uncooperative underlings, and to enjoy some swigging time with the only people who truly get you: Real Men.

PROSPERO'S DARK AND STORMY

Imagine yourself lounging on the sands of your very own island, conjuring up storms to terrorize your enemies, and being waited on hand and foot by a pair of indentured servants. Not a bad gig if you can get it—just ask Prospero from *The Tempest*. After his brother unseats him as Duke of Milan and sends him off to sea with his toddler daughter, Prospero does some usurping of his own. When he and Miranda land on a remote island, Prospero uses the sadistic abracadabra he's been studying to enslave the natives, Caliban and Ariel. Now he's the ruler of a whole kingdom! After a few of these tropical cold ones, you'll definitely believe in

MINI-BARD

Going off on a sea expedition, conquering a "new" world, and enslaving its natives was a great way to get Man points in Shakespeare's time. *The Tempest* was likely inspired by the 1609 shipwreck of an English vessel going on just such a mission. The passengers were heading to join the Jamestown, Virginia, settlement, but ended up on the shores of the Bermuda islands—a place a lot like the paradise Prospero steals from Caliban. European explorers of the Americas often kidnapped natives and brought them home to put on display for money, or to give as gifts to their monarchs. In *The Tempest*, the servant Stephano hopes to up his status in this way when he first sees Caliban: "If I can recover him and keep him tame and get to Naples with him, he's a present for any emperor." Dream on, Stephano. Prospero already owns this island—and everyone on it.

your own superhuman powers. Just don't try to fly. You might break your magic staff.

> 2 thin disks fresh ginger
> 2 ounces dark rum (preferably Gosling's Black Seal Bermuda)
> 5 ounces ginger beer
> Lime wedge

Place the ginger disks in a highball glass and muddle to create an ominous cloudy effect. Fill the glass with ice. Pour in the rum and ginger beer, and stir. Garnish with a lime wedge. Feel the power.

HENRY VIII'S WHISKEY SLASH

The best leaders aren't afraid to make unpopular decisions. Like King Henry VIII, if you're a Real Man you have to be ready to ditch a pope, behead a wife who can't give you a male heir, or divorce one who's just kind of ugly. In *Henry VIII*, or *All Is True*, Shakespeare and his cowriter John Fletcher dramatized the king's smooth Man-euvering from Wife #1 to Wife #2. Breaking up is hard to do, but only if you're a pussy. This whiskey cocktail celebrates the alpha male's right to slash any inconvenient ties that bind. Like a sacrament. Or a neck.

> 10 fresh mint leaves
> ½ cup lemon pieces
> ½ ounce simple syrup
> 2½ ounces rye whiskey
> Maraschino cherries

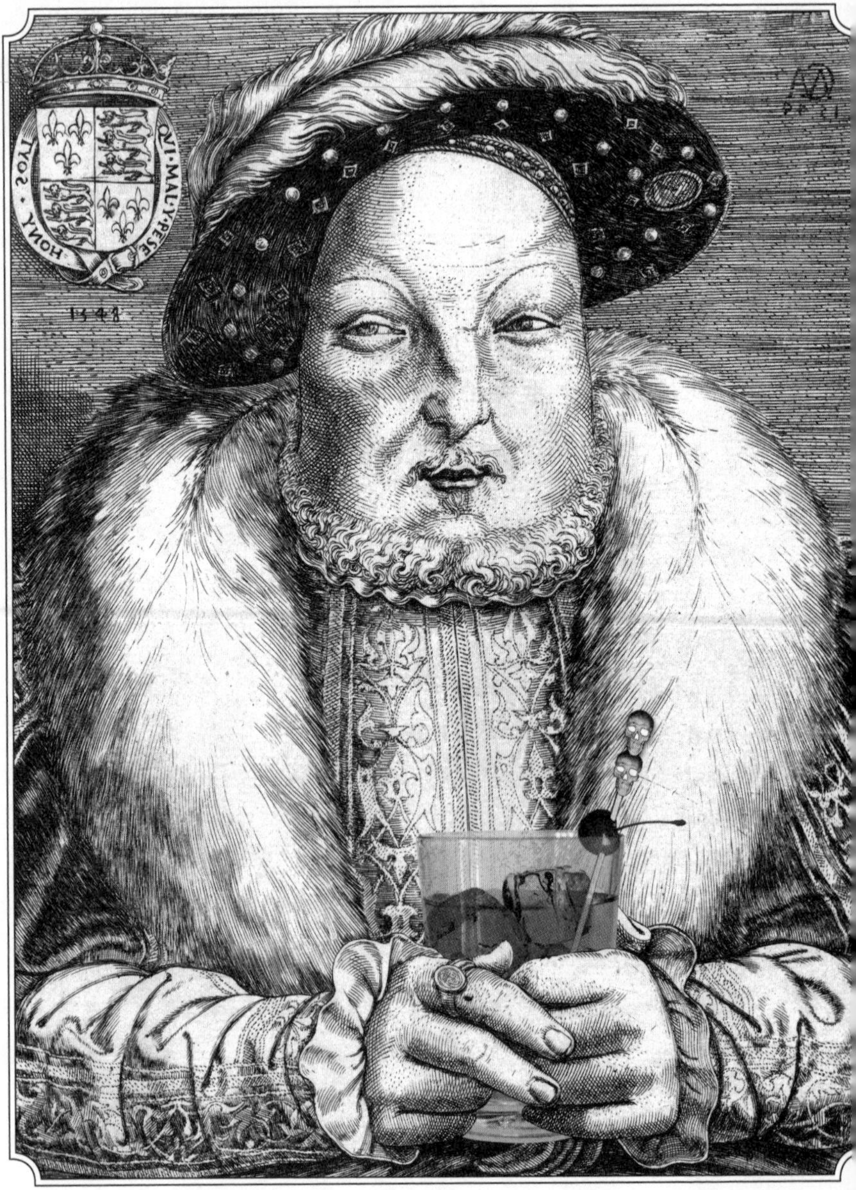
QVI · MALY · PESE
HONY · SOYT
1548

MINI-BARD

Henry VIII broke the Man-o-Meter when he split from the pope *and* his first wife, Catherine of Aragon—all so that he could marry his mistress Anne Boleyn. Henry and his team started weakening Rome's power in England by getting a series of Acts passed in 1532 (when it was looking like Henry was never going to get the divorce or the son he wanted). They completed the break with Rome two years later when Henry declared himself Supreme Head of the Church of England. In the meantime, he'd already married the pregnant Anne and gotten the Archbishop of Canterbury to nullify his marriage to Catherine. The play *Henry VIII* casts Anne as "the goodliest woman / That ever lay by man," and ends with the christening of her and Henry's baby daughter, the future Queen Elizabeth I. The playwrights didn't include any of that messy later stuff about Anne getting beheaded when she, like Catherine, failed to produce a male heir. Or anything about Henry's other (*cough*) four wives. The original Globe Theatre burned to the ground during a 1613 performance of *Henry VIII* when a cannon shot, meant to herald the king's greatness in act 1, blew up in his face. Can you say "karma"?

Slash the mint leaves into little pieces. In a shaker, muddle the lemon pieces with the mint leaves and the simple syrup until they cry out for mercy. Add ice and the whiskey. Shake *hard* and strain into an old-fashioned glass over ice. Stick 3 (or more, if you're feeling the urge) maraschino cherry "heads" on an olive pick, for garnish.

ANTONY'S FUZZY NAVAL

First rule in the *Real Man Handbook*: Never let your woman break up your band. There's no surer way to lose the respect of your guy friends and coworkers. Not to mention your half of the Roman Empire. If only Antony had taken the advice of his military bro-horts in *Antony and Cleopatra* and stuck to his strength: fighting on land. Instead, he lets his girlfriend, Cleopatra, convince him to fight his Roman rival Octavian at sea. She contributes a fleet of her own but then decides to leave at the height of the battle, taking all of her ships with her. And Antony's so fuzzy about his naval priorities that he follows her! Octavian gets to become the all-powerful emperor Caesar Augustus, while Antony's loss at the Battle of Actium tanks his military and political future and goes down in history as one of the most humiliating maritime defeats ever. Shakespeare really plays up Antony's unmanliness when he has the soldier Scarus describe him as a "doting mallard" flying after Cleopatra: "I never saw an action of such shame. / Experience, manhood, honour, ne'er before / Did violate so itself." Ouch. Lesson learned: listen to your wingman, or end up a lame duck.

Like Antony, we've screwed up the standard "naval" formation by reversing the orange juice and peach schnapps elements. But our orange liqueur and peach nectar, finished with sea salt and foam (prosecco), is definitely a winning strategy.

> Lemon wedge
> Fine sea salt
> ¼ cup peach nectar
> ½ ounce Cointreau
> ½ ounce Grand Marnier
> 1 teaspoon fresh lemon juice
> Splash of prosecco
> Peach slice

Rim a highball glass with a lemon wedge and dip the rim in salt. Fill the glass halfway with ice. Add the peach nectar, Cointreau, Grand

Marnier, and lemon juice, and stir. Top with prosecco and garnish with a peach slice.

~❧~

IAGO'S CON-I-KAZE

When the boss passes you over for that big promotion and gives it to the Ivy League pretender in the next cubicle, you don't curl up in a ball and sob like a girl-baby. No way. If you're like Iago, General Othello's jealous underling, you quietly plot the destruction of all things good in the world. When *Othello* begins, Iago is furious that the general has picked Michael Cassio—an "arithmetician" who "never set a squadron in the field"—as his lieutenant instead of him. So he hatches a complicated series of cons, all designed to ruin both of his nemeses. First Iago gets Cassio drunk on the job and fired. Then he convinces Cassio to ask Desdemona, Othello's new wife, to help him get his job back. All of that cozying up to the boss's woman sets the stage for Iago's biggest con yet: convincing Othello that Cassio's sleeping with her and that he should strangle her in "the bed she hath contaminated," leaving Iago to be Cassio's "undertaker." After whipping Othello up into a homicidal rage, Iago sits back and lets the *merda* hit the fan. By the end of the play, most of the good characters (including Othello, Desdemona, and Iago's wife, Emilia) are dead and Iago's arrested. He has no regrets, but *you* may want to think twice before deciding to "pour this pestilence" into your boss's ear. We recommend pouring yourself one of these Con-i-kazes instead. It may not give you the same misanthropic rush, but it'll dull the pain of mediocrity and let you keep your retirement bennies.

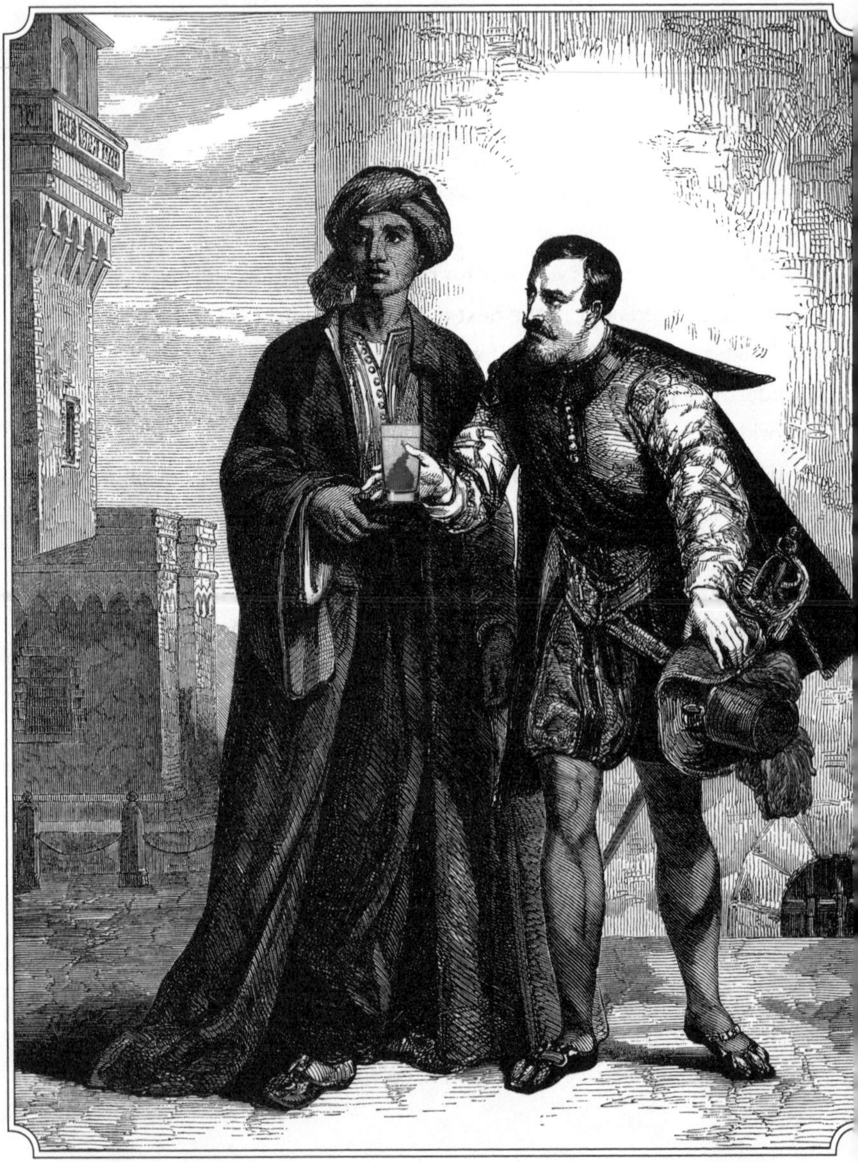

1 ounce triple sec

1 ounce vodka

¾ ounce fresh lime juice

⅓ ounce Grand Marnier

Shake the triple sec, vodka, and lime with ice. Strain into a cold, unfeeling martini glass. In the center of the drink, drizzle in the Grand Marnier, slowly and secretly. Like pestilence, it starts as a subtle fog and then packs its punch. Your guests will never know what hit them.

✎ SAVORY MATTERS ✐

MAKI-BETH ROLLS

Macbeth loses his job and his head faster than you can say "Highlander," so it's easy to forget that when *Macbeth* begins, he's the Big Man on the Battlefield. Even before he sets foot onstage, his army comrades are raving about how he sliced open a Scottish traitor "from the nave to th' chops." His sword was so full of man-heat that it "smoked with bloody execution"! True, Macbeth may have made a slight error in judgment later with that regicide incident, but he earned his original reputation as a military badass fair and square. If you're sick of people dumping on your legacy because of one lousy mistake, let Macbeth's "smoked" Scottish salmon maki rouse your taste buds and remind you of the days when your love of raw flesh brought kudos, not condemnation.

• *40 rolls*

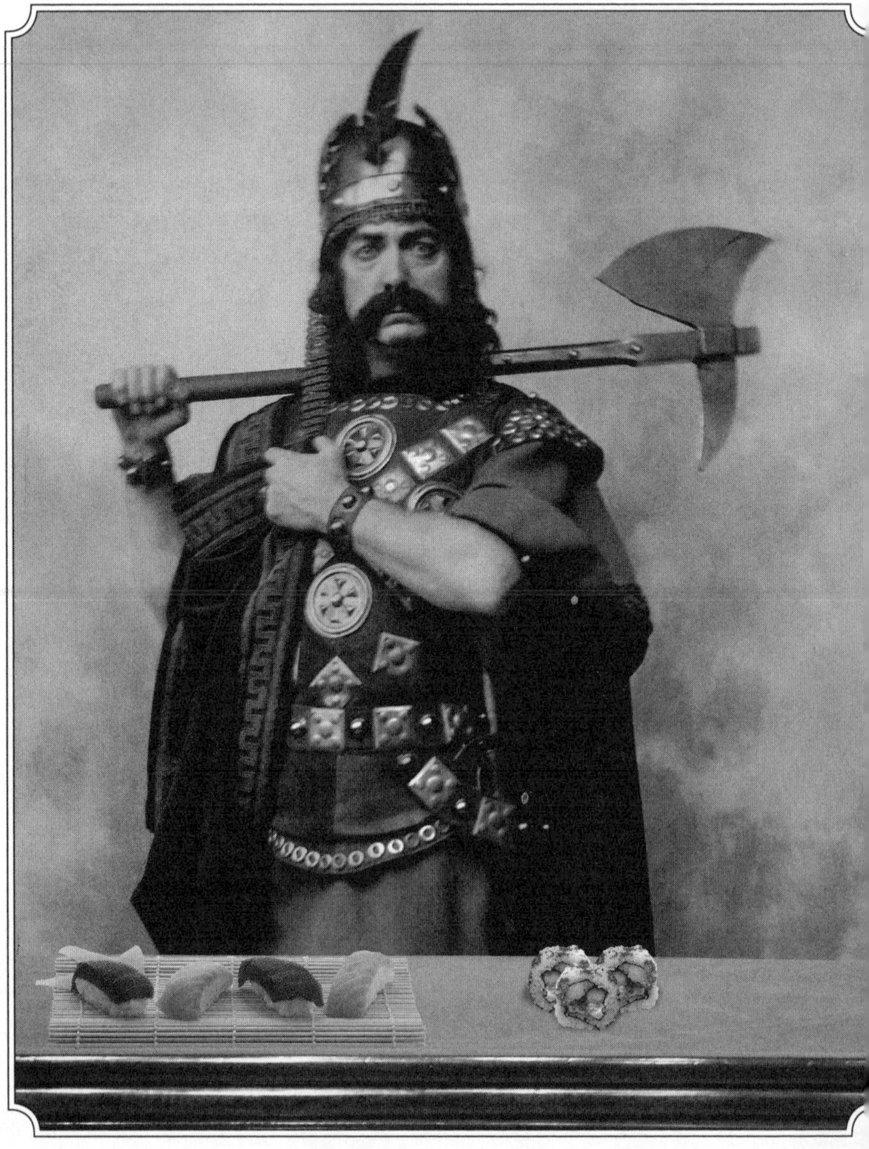

2 cups uncooked sushi rice

2 tablespoons seasoned rice vinegar

1½ tablespoons wasabi paste

4 ounces sour cream

8 roasted nori (seaweed) sheets

8 ounces smoked Scottish salmon, cut into thin strips

1 English cucumber, peeled, halved, seeded, and cut lengthwise
    into ¼-inch-thick strips

8 ounces salmon roe

Black sesame seeds

Prepare the rice according to the package instructions. When fully cooked, stir in the rice vinegar and set aside to cool in a bowl, covered with a cloth. Prepare wasabi cream by mixing the wasabi and sour cream in small bowl. On bamboo mat, place one sheet of nori (rough side facing upward) and cover with a thin layer of rice, leaving a 1-inch margin on the bottom. Lay a strip of smoked salmon across the middle of the rice and spread with a spoonful of wasabi cream. Next to the smoked salmon, place a strip of cucumber. Roll the maki all the way up, sealing the nori flap with dabs of cold water. Dip your smoking sword or serrated knife into cold water and *ARRARGHNNARRGH!* into 6 pieces. Repeat with the rest of the nori. Top each maki piece with a small spoonful of roe and a sprinkling of sesame seeds.

BERTRAM'S CRUSHED NUTS

Bertram's got big dreams in *All's Well That Ends Well*. If only he could turn twenty-one and finally claim his dad's estate. Instead, he has to be a ward of the crown and do everything the king tells him to do. Like marry that pathetic girl Helena and hang around playing husband while his buddies get to become Real Men on the battlefield. As his best friend, Parolles, says, "A young man married is a man that's marred." *Yeah! That's right! To hell with the king! I'm never sleeping with Helena! I'm gonna sneak off to war, shoot a bunch of stuff, and have all the one-night stands I want!* Whoa. Slow down, there, young Bertram. The Testosterone Train is about to grind to a humiliating halt when Helena swaps places with your girlfriend, tricks you into consummating your marriage, and then exposes you as a lying douche bag in front of everyone. Including your mommy. But your pain is our readers' gain—because all's well that ends with this nuts-based party mix that's fun to chomp into little bits!   • *2½ cups*

½ cup roasted, unsalted peanuts

½ cup cashews

½ cup roasted, salted pepitas

Olive oil spray

Sea salt

½ cup raisins

½ cup coarsely chopped dried figs

1 dried fig, quartered

Preheat the oven to 350°F. In a bowl, mix the peanuts, cashews, and pepitas. Spread the mixture evenly on a baking sheet, coat lightly with olive oil spray, and sprinkle with sea salt. Bake for 10 to 12 minutes. Let cool. Combine with the raisins and chopped figs in a small bowl. Garnish with extra fig quarters.

TITUS'S MINI MEAT PIES

Are you mad as hell and not going to take it anymore? Titus of *Titus Andronicus* fame knows just how you feel—and then some. After serving as general of the Roman army and sacrificing twenty-one of his sons to fighting the barbarous Goths, Titus gets dropped by his new emperor-boss, kills one of his own sons, suffers the violation of his only daughter and the beheading of two more sons, and then gets tricked into chopping off his own hand. And that's just in the first three acts. The Goth queen, Tamora, and her co-conspirators may have taken his and his family's body parts, but they didn't break the old codger's spirit. After pouring all his manhood into serving the Roman state, Titus puts his heart and soul (well, actually the hearts and heads of Tamora's sons) into the meat pies he serves up to her before announcing that she's "eating the flesh that she herself hath bred." *Gotcha!* No one was harmed in the preparation of our version, but we've kept Titus's hot-blooded vengeance cooked into every bite.   • *25–30 hors d'oeuvres*

    ½ onion, minced
    3 cloves garlic, minced
    1 tablespoon olive oil
    1 pound hot Italian sausage
    ¼ cup white wine

continued...

¼ cup heavy cream

2 tablespoons whole-grain Dijon mustard

¼ cup chopped basil

MINI-BARD Shakespeare's earliest tragedy and bloodiest slashfest, *Titus Andronicus* was a sensation when it first hit the stage around 1594. But it fell out of favor over the next four centuries. T. S. Eliot declared it "one of the stupidest and most uninspired plays ever written," and Harold Bloom called it a "poetic atrocity." Such an atrocity, in fact, that many eighteenth- and nineteenth-century critics, from Alexander Pope to Samuel Taylor Coleridge, denied Shakespeare wrote it at all (or claimed that he just helped touch it up). But revenge dramas, with their disembodied heads and limbs, were all the rage in Shakespeare's day. So was Arthur Golding's 1567 translation of Ovid's *Metamorphoses*, a collection of myths full of sex, violence, and violent sex. Shakespeare capitalized on the popularity of both with *Titus*, basing his revenge tragedy on the Ovidian tale of Philomela's rape by her sister Procne's husband. Procne punishes him by baking their only son into a pie and feeding it to him. Shakespeare reworks the story and doubles the gore factor: Titus serves up his daughter Lavinia's two rapists to their mother, Tamora, because she had egged them on to violate Lavinia—*her* act of revenge against Titus, who let his son lop off *her* son's limbs and throw his entrails into the fire at the start of the play. This part happens *before* Tamora tries to hide her adultery by attempting to kill the love child she has with Aaron the Moor. *He*'s the one who first hatches the plan for Tamora's sons to rape Lavinia and kill her husband. And then frame two of Titus's sons for the murder with some buried treasure, a fake note, and a booby-trap hole. That's when Aaron tricks Titus into chopping off his hand to save their lives but gives him their heads instead. Which of course leads to Titus making Lavinia carry his hand around in her mouth, because . . . wait a minute. Maybe Shakespeare *didn't* write this.

¼ teaspoon red pepper flakes

1 package frozen mini phyllo cups, thawed

Sour cream

In a large skillet, sauté the onion and garlic in the oil over medium heat until golden. Remove from the pan and set aside. Take the sausages out of their casings and add to the pan, breaking them up into small pieces. Cook through over medium heat. Add white wine and simmer until reduced by half. Add in heavy cream, mustard, basil, red pepper, and reserved onion and garlic. Stir until thickened, about 3 minutes. Fill the phyllo cups with the sausage mixture and top with the a small dab of sour cream. Serve immediately.

OBERON'S SPICY FAIRY WINGS WITH BLUE CHEESE DIP OF DOMINATION

When we first meet King Oberon and Queen Titania in *A Midsummer Night's Dream*, they're in an epic domestic battle. Oberon demands to have the little Indian boy that Titania's deceased disciple entrusted her to raise, but Titania refuses to give him up. She confronts Oberon with her fairy minions and announces that, until he backs off, she's "forsworn his bed and company." But no one—not even a queen—comes between Oberon and what he wants. Especially if they're the cloyingly cute fairies who support his estranged wife. *What's that, little Peaseblossom? Sorry, I can't hear you. Did you say that you wanted your sweet little wings ripped off, baked, and smothered in the Blue Cheese Dip of Domination?*

• *6 servings*

BLUE CHEESE DIP OF DOMINATION

1 cup crumbled blue cheese

½ cup sour cream

¼ cup mayonnaise

1 teaspoon Worcestershire sauce

1 teaspoon fresh lemon juice

Salt, to taste

1 cup all-purpose flour

¾ teaspoon garlic powder

¾ teaspoon salt

2 pounds chicken wings

Nonstick cooking spray

½ cup hot pepper sauce

Prepare the dipping sauce by combining all ingredients in a small bowl. Cover and refrigerate.

Put the flour, garlic powder, and salt in a ziplock bag and shake until blended. Add the wings and shake until coated. Take out the wings and refrigerate for an hour. Preheat the oven to 400°F. Coat a cooling rack with nonstick spray and place it on a cookie sheet. Put the wings on the rack and bake for 25 minutes. Turn and bake for 15 more minutes. Take the wings out and dip them in the hot pepper sauce. Return to the oven for 10 more minutes. Remove from the oven, cool, and get the dip out of the refrigerator. Prepare to plunge the wings into submission.

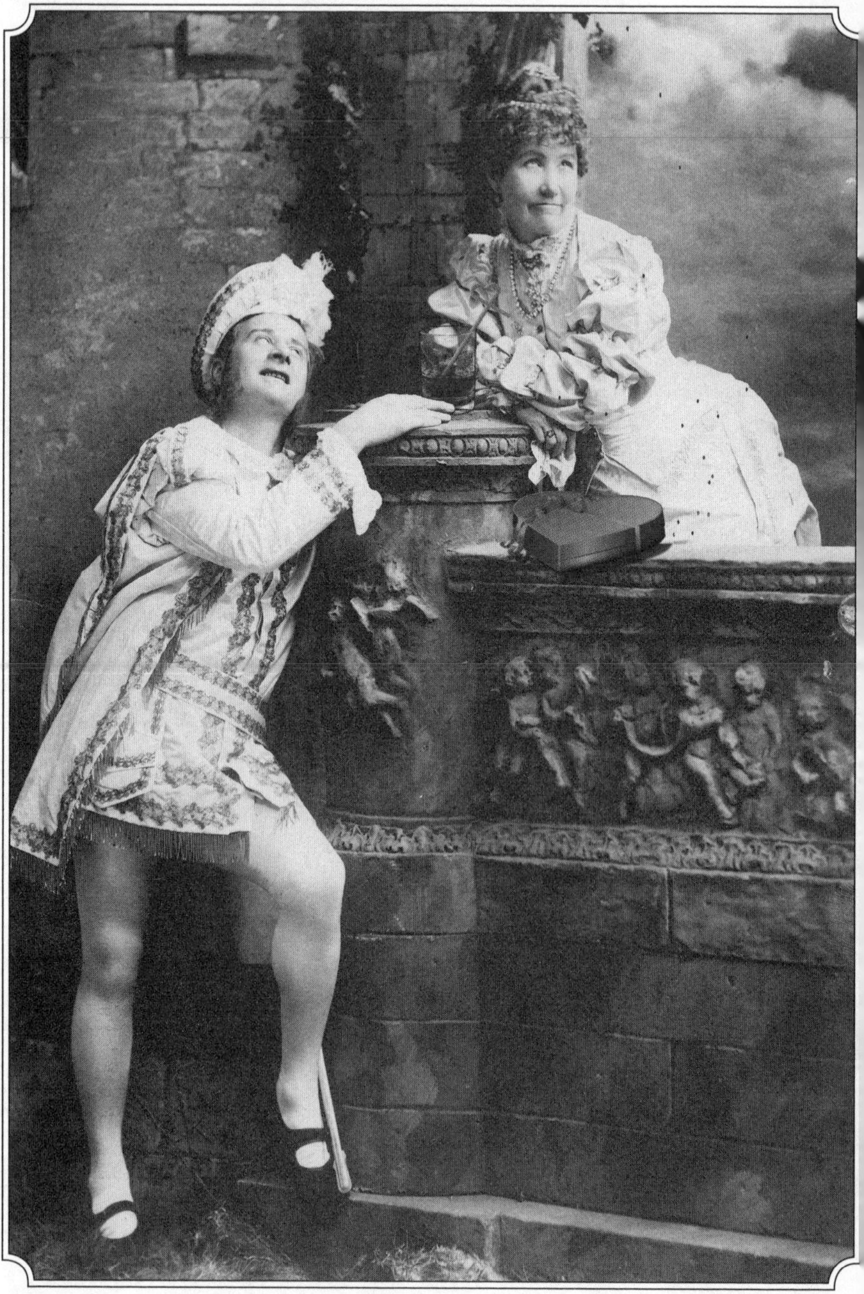

Shall I Campari
to a Summer's Day?

Romantic Occasions

hakespeare knew that "the course of true love never did run
smooth"—which is why we've made these cocktails sweet, sour,
bitter, and straight-up strange. They're full of surprises, just like
Love itself. The speaker of Shakespeare's sonnets tries to hold on to his
beloved young man by praising him with "eternal lines" of poetry—like
"Shall I compare thee to a summer's day?"—but he still gets his heart
broken. Whether it's fickle lovers, mystery bed partners, or sexy beasts
of burden, you never know what Cupid has in store. Or what obstacles
you'll face: fear of commitment, disapproving parents, donkey/fairy language barriers, what have you. Whether you're looking to spice things
up or cool things down, these concoctions are for all you lovers out there
looking to celebrate your special chemistry.

⚓ COCKTAILS ⚓

ROSALIND'S GENDER BLENDER

Are things getting too predictable with your significant other? Maybe it's time for some role-playing. For a lot of Shakespeare's characters, cross-dressing and gender mash-ups are the stuff of everyday erotica. And no character mixes it up better than Rosalind in *As You Like It*. She dresses up like a young man and then names herself "Ganymede" (Zeus's boy-toy cupbearer) before going off in pursuit of Orlando. Adding to the gender-bending fun, all of the girl characters would have been played by boy actors since Englishwomen weren't accepted on the public stage until 1660. So, really, every Shakespearean girl turned boy is a boy turned girl turned boy who eventually turns girl again even though she's really a boy. You know what? Just enjoy this sweet blended concoction with your partner and try not to think too hard about it.

> 2 ounces vodka
> ½ cup lemon sorbet
> ½ cup frozen raspberries
> ½ cup frozen blueberries
> ¼ cup simple syrup
> ¼ cup white wine
> Fresh blueberries, for garnish

In a blender, puree the vodka, lemon sorbet, frozen raspberries, frozen blueberries, simple syrup, and white wine until pink and blue become a purple blur. Pour into a heavy wineglass or goblet and top with fresh blueberries. Serve immediately.

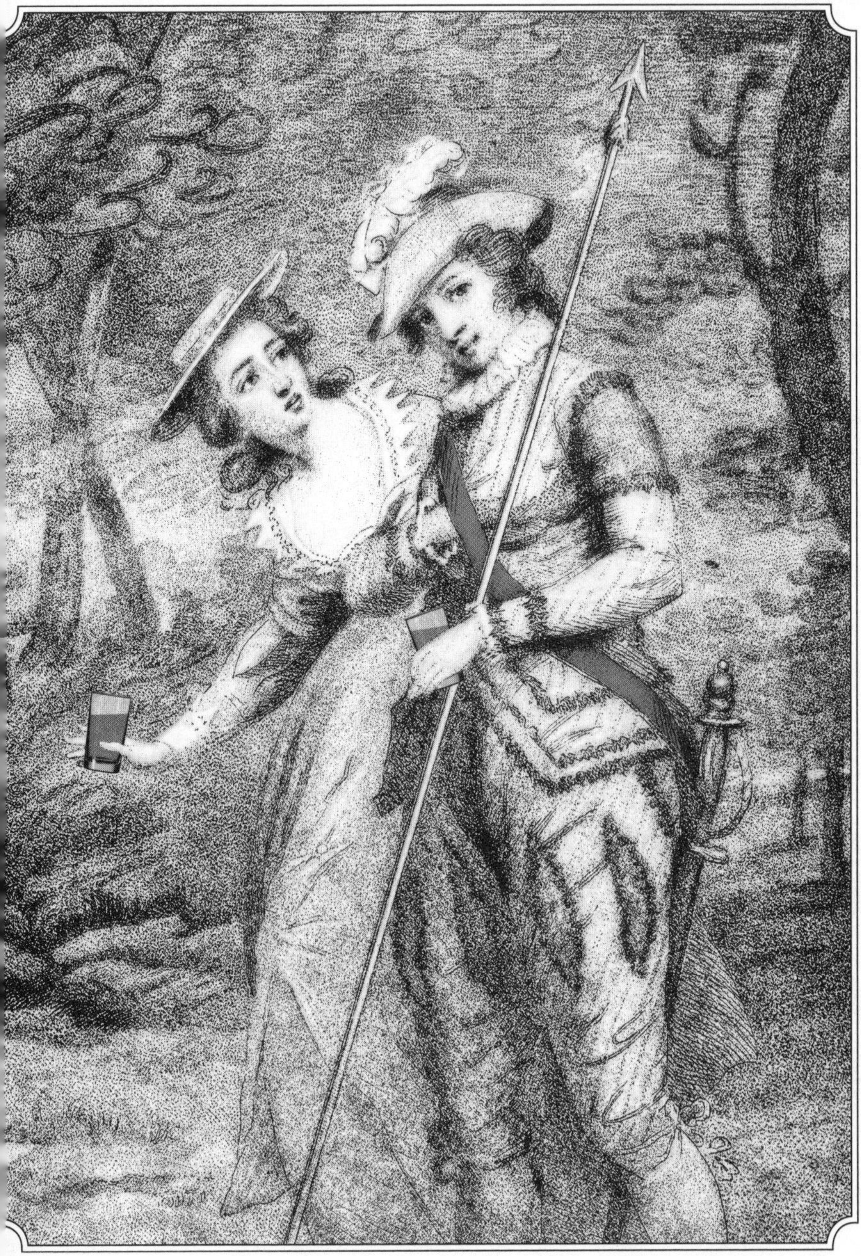

Rosalind isn't the only girl to go boy and find love. *Twelfth Night*'s Viola puts on pants to work for Orsino, and then falls hard for him; Jessica dresses like a boy so she can elope with Lorenzo in *The Merchant of Venice*; and Julia poses as a page to hunt down her boyfriend, Proteus, in *The Two Gentlemen of Verona*. Sometimes boys go girl, but it's usually not very romantic. The Page in *The Taming of the Shrew* is forced by his master to put on a dress and pretend to be a drunk guy's wife; and Cleopatra speaks disdainfully of the "squeaking" prepubescent actor who would "boy my greatness" for the Roman riffraff. Not that a guy dressing up like her *couldn't* be hot given the right situation. Like the night she got Antony drunk, dressed him up in her "tires and mantles," and strapped on his sword. *Me-ow.*

HELENA'S RASPBERRY LIME MICKEY

Shakespeare's comedies always end in promises of marriage. But sometimes the men need a little (**ahem**) *nudge* when it comes to making that big commitment. Remember the triple wedding at the end of *A Midsummer Night's Dream*? Guess who didn't: Demetrius, Helena's groom. When they say their "I do's," he's still under the influence of the magic flower juice Puck put on his eyes to make him love her. But let's not let a little thing like entrapment get in the way of a happy ending. It definitely didn't stop the other Helena (from *All's Well That Ends Well*) from bed-tricking her runaway husband, Bertram, into sleeping with her and knocking her up. While we don't advocate the use of hallucinogens or body doubles to procure an engagement ring or a Perma-Spouse, this drink might help loosen up that commitment-phobe of yours.

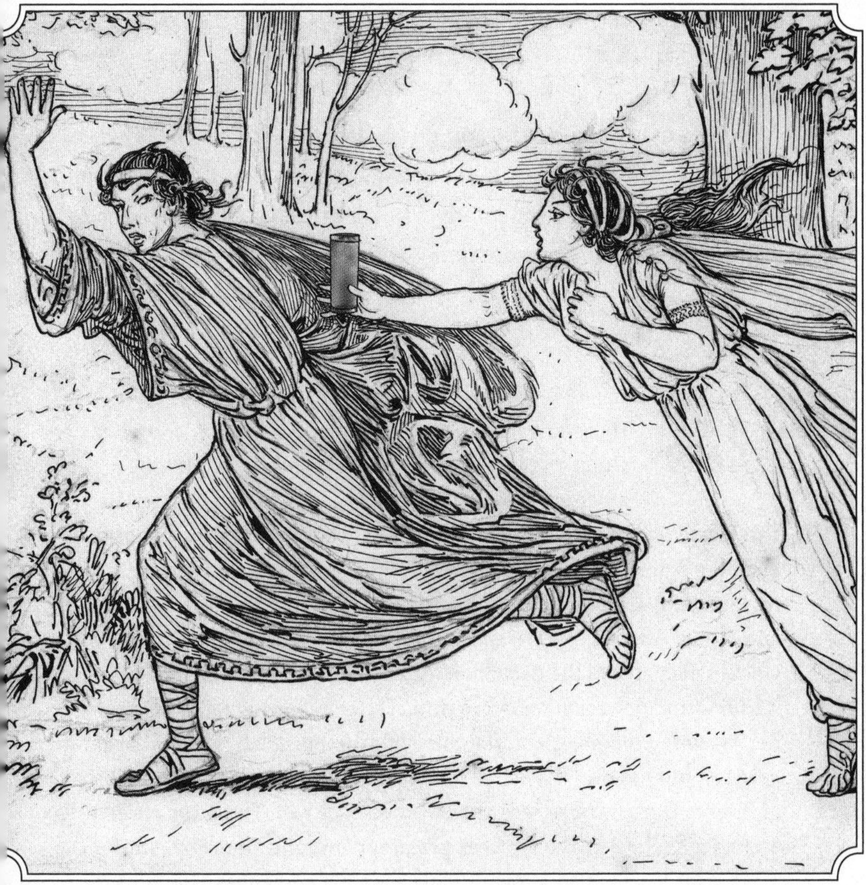

4 fresh raspberries

2 lime slices

3 ounces Absolut Raspberri vodka

¼ cup fresh lime juice

½ ounce simple syrup

Splash of seltzer

Muddle 2 of the raspberries and 1 lime slice together in a heavy glass. Fill the glass with ice and stir in the vodka, lime juice, and simple syrup. Top with seltzer and the remaining 2 raspberries. Garnish with the remaining slice of lime. Start dreaming about seating charts.

MINI-BARD

The bed-trick—a sexual scenario in which someone switches places with one of the partners without the other partner knowing—has a long literary history. Laban swaps Rachel out for Leah on Jacob's wedding night in Genesis; and King Arthur is conceived when Uther Pendragon pulls a switcheroo on Igraine. But bed-tricks didn't appear on the English stage until the late 1590s. And *All's Well That Ends Well* was one of the first to put a woman in charge of the deception. After Bertram dumps Helena post-wedding and pre-consummation with a letter telling her he'll never call her his wife until she's carrying his child (*Impossible!*), Helena takes matters into her own hands. She joins forces with Bertram's would-be girlfriend, Diana, who agrees to be the bed-trick bait. This gives Helena a chance to take Diana's place, get pregnant, and trap Bertram for good. *Ha!* It's hard to know if Shakespeare's audiences would have been *Fatal Attraction* scared by this girl-power plotline, or *Legally Blonde* psyched about it. But it seems to have started a trend, appearing multiple times in other playwrights' works over the next forty years.

MUCH ADO ABOUT FROTHING

Before there was Hepburn and Tracy, or Liz and Dick, there was *Much Ado About Nothing*'s volatile couple, Beatrice and Benedick. At first, the two committed singletons spend all their time shooting witty barbs at each other across Tuscan lemon orchards and declaring their mutual hatred. Beatrice calls him a "stuffed man" (read: dummy); Benedick dubs her the bitchy "Lady Disdain." But there was some real chemistry behind those explosive exchanges. Because by the end of the play, they're madly in love! This fizzy concoction, inspired by the pisco sour, brings you the traditional lemon flavor of the romantic Italian countryside with a frothy kick in honor of Beatrice and Benedick's biting repartee. If you enjoy the fiery thrill of dramatic fights and hot make-up sessions, mix up one of these and enjoy. But, please, keep it indoors.

2½ ounces pisco
¾ ounce fresh lemon juice
1 egg white
½ ounce simple syrup
2–3 dashes Angostura bitters
Edible heart sprinkles

Pour the pisco, lemon juice, egg white, and simple syrup into a shaker with ice and shake hard for 20 seconds. Strain into a martini glass. Finish with a few dashes of bitters. Top with edible heart sprinkles. Enjoy the fireworks!

A MIDSUMMER NIGHT'S BEAN DIP

This combo of humble beans and upscale truffle oil is inspired by the lowly weaver Bottom and Queen Titania's midsummer night's dream hookup in her luxury forest bower. The donkey-headed weaver from the other side of the tracks gets a taste of the good life—scalp massages and all-night hay and honey-bag deliveries; and Fairy Queen Titania learns the true meaning of getting *down*. Like the time you went to Club Med Punta Cana with your family and met Pascal, the trapeze instructor's son. You taught him the difference between sushi and sashimi; he swept you off your Burberry sandals, flew you to the stars, and made you feel *alive*. It was never going to last, and neither will this dip.   • *2 cups*

> 1 (16-ounce) can cannellini beans, drained
>
> 3 cloves garlic, peeled and crushed
>
> 8 ounces smoked trout
>
> ½ cup chopped parsley
>
> ¼ teaspoon salt
>
> ¼ teaspoon pepper
>
> 3 tablespoons truffle-infused oil
>
> 1 baguette, thinly sliced

Place all ingredients except the baguette in a food processor and puree. Serve in bowl surrounded by baguette slices.

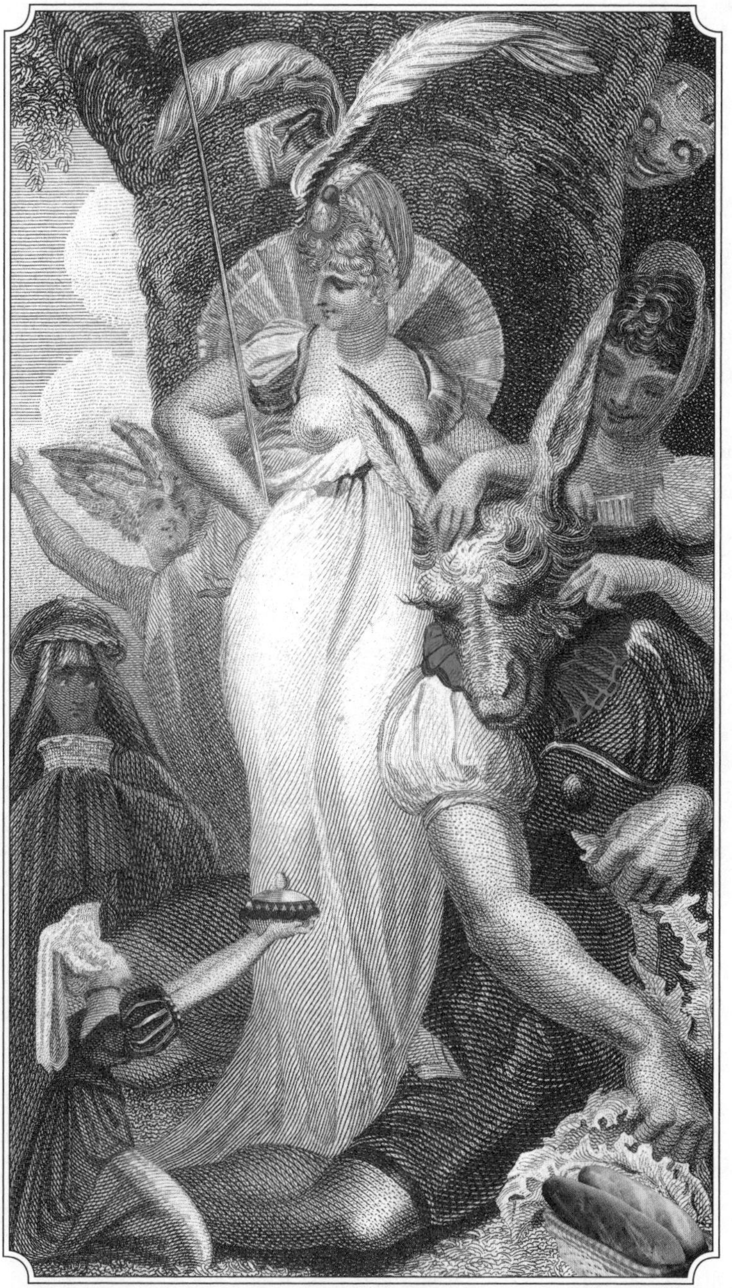

PORTIA'S BOX

Despite major obstacles, you're *finally* with your one true love. *The Merchant of Venice*'s Portia and Bassanio would definitely appreciate this celebration. Portia's father is intent on controlling his daughter's future—even though he's dead. He leaves behind a will that obligates her to marry the first man who can pass his Super Secret Test. It involves three boxes (gold, silver, and lead), each with its own cryptic inscription. A suitor gets only one shot to select the winning box with Portia's picture inside. Pick it and you get Portia, her money, and the whole Belmont Estate. Pick one of the other two boxes, though, and you can never get married to anyone. Ever. Portia and Bassanio (the only guy she actually likes) endure a real nail-biter when he tries to get into her box. Er, anyway . . . it's an enormous relief when Bassanio rejects the "tainted

MINI-BARD Portia's complaint—"I may neither choose who I would nor refuse who I dislike"—wasn't totally unreasonable. The traditional model of male authority where women had to obey fathers and husbands was certainly alive and well when Shakespeare wrote *Merchant*, but marriage advice books were also starting to talk about the benefits of mutual affection and respect. When husband and wife understood each other as domestic partners, they had a better chance at a healthy and holy matrimony. Like the writer of *Counsel to the Husband* (1608) says: spousal fighting is the "Canker unto happiness" and can be avoided if couples maintain a "joint governing of their family" and if "true regard be had unto mutual duty." Someone raise this guy from the dead and get him an agent! We smell an Oprah endorsement.

and corrupt" gold and "common" silver boxes to open Portia's modest lead box. Wait, no. What we mean is: With these box-themed sandwiches, you can ~~have all the boxes you want! eat fresh boxes morning, noon, and night!~~ relish your love's victory over the random, stressful tests thrown your way. Especially ones where your father makes guys solve riddles about your box. Crap. • *6 servings*

6 tablespoons sesame oil

10 ounces shiitake mushrooms

½ cup chopped walnuts

3 tablespoons fresh lemon juice

1 teaspoon fresh thyme

2 cloves garlic, peeled and crushed

Salt and pepper, to taste

Rectangular-shaped crackers

Coarsely chop the mushrooms and sauté in sesame oil until soft. Pour the mushrooms and pan oil into a food processor. Add the remaining ingredients except the crackers and puree. Serve on crackers. Or something else that looks like a box. We're going to stop talking about this recipe now.

LOVE'S LABOUR'S
TOTS WITH AGED CHEESE

Unlike your friends who've sprinted to the altar, you two have taken your slow, sweet time. Just like the couples at the end of *Love's Labour's Lost*, you've let your love age a bit before rushing to commit. Before they make the "world-without-end bargain" of marriage, the pragmatic Princess of France and her three ladies-in-waiting ask their suitors to wait a year. That way, everyone can be sure that true fidelity lies behind the whispered sweet nothings of new romance. When *you* finally come to that mature, surprise-free union, you'll want to celebrate it with this familiar comfort food, garnished with aged Parmesan. Because now you know what you like, and you'll never get tired of it. Like your long-term partner. And potatoes.

• *12–15 hors d'oeuvres*

1 large russet potato, peeled and quartered
½ cup freshly grated aged Parmesan
2 teaspoons salt
½ teaspoon pepper
Panko bread crumbs
Canola oil spray

Boil the potato in salted water until soft enough to mash. Remove and let cool. While the potato cools, preheat the oven to 450°F. Mash together the potato, Parmesan, salt, and pepper. Mold into teaspoon-size "tot" cylinders and dredge in panko crumbs. Arrange the tots on a cookie sheet lined with aluminum foil. Spray liberally with canola oil and bake for 15 minutes, until crispy and golden brown. Serve with the comfort dip of your choice.

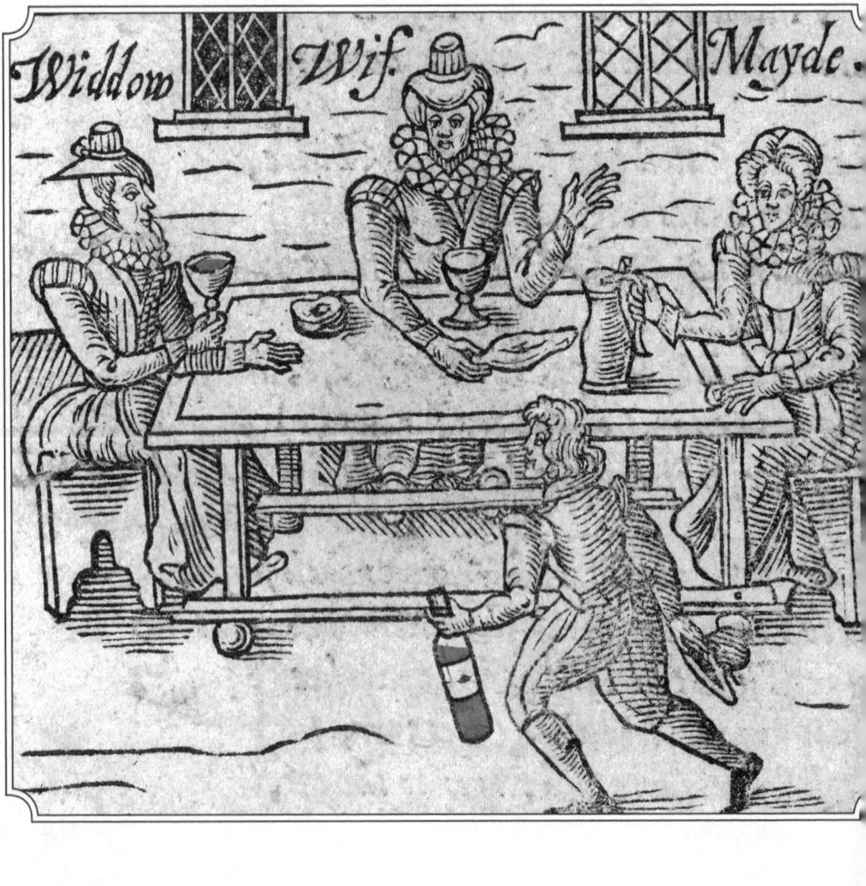
Widdow
Wif.
Mayde

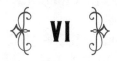

VI

Get Thee to a Winery

Girls' Night Out

When Hamlet tells Ophelia to "Get thee to a nunnery," he's either calling her a whore (*nunnery* was also slang for *brothel*) or he's living in a fantasy world. By the time Shakespeare was writing, English *and* Danish convents were a thing of the past. Instead of being chaste, silent, and obedient at the local abbey, all kinds of single ladies were out and about—working retail in the new London shops, sewing and cooking for rich people, lactating for lucre, running small businesses, and planning Women's Weekends in man-bashing Amazon country. (Okay, maybe not that last one.) The fact is, most English-women weren't getting married until their midtwenties, and a lot of them never did. These fun-loving singletons are everywhere in Shakespeare's world, and they're headed straight to the winery, where they can swap sex tips, make fun of their ex-boyfriends, and buy everyone a round on their dead husbands' shilling.

THE NURSE'S SLIPPERY WORMWOOD NIPPLE

Merry widows are always up for a good time. Now that they're free of those pesky doctrines about wifely compliance, they can run off at the mouth all they want. Plus they know everything about sex, so they can tell virgins how great it is and encourage all kinds of fun, bad behavior. Juliet's Nurse is the queen of inappropriate body-talk, especially when she yammers on about boobs and Juliet's sex life in front of the repressed Lady Capulet. Our take on the Slippery Nipple is based on the Nurse's fabulously cringe-worthy speech about weaning Juliet: she "did taste the wormwood on the nipple / Of my dug and felt it bitter." Yikes. You're going to need this Nipple just to get *that* one out of your head. The only upside to Juliet not getting the wedding of her dreams is that her Nurse won't get a chance to grab the mic.

½ ounce sambuca
½ ounce Baileys Irish Cream
3 dashes wormwood bitters
Drop of grenadine

Pour the sambuca into a shot glass. Carefully layer the Irish cream on top by pouring it over the back of a spoon. Add the bitters. Tilt the glass slightly and slip the grenadine in at the lower edge to produce a "nipple" effect. Latch on and suck it down—before it's gone for good.

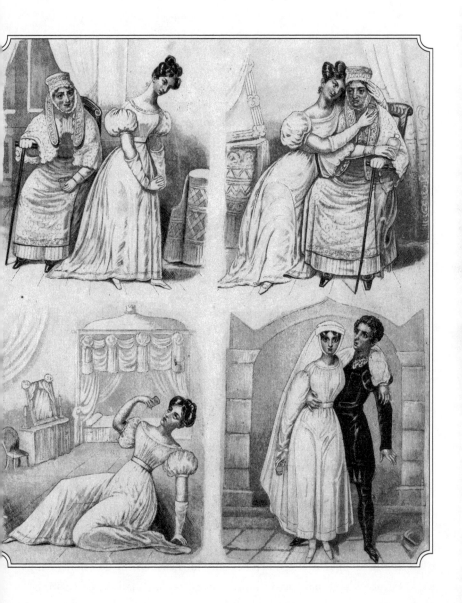

MINI-BARD The Nurse is thrilled to remind Juliet's mother that she was the one who nursed Juliet for years while Mr. and Mrs. Capulet did things like go on couples' retreats to Lake Como. It was typical for upper-class ladies (and other new mothers who could afford it) to employ their social inferiors as wet-nurses. Having a wet-nurse wasn't just a status symbol and a way to preserve your perky breasts; upper-class husbands were psyched about hiring them, too, since it made their wives more available for churning out valuable little heirs. The only trouble was, people believed women passed along all kinds of dodgy stuff through their milk—not just diseases, but sluttiness, devil worship, and low-class accents. Puritan ministers started an anti-wet-nursing movement in the early 1600s that criticized gentlewomen who were too selfish to take care of their own kids and protect the purity of England's most precious offspring. But that was waaaaaaay back in the olden days when people made lots of judgments about women and blamed the downfall of civilization on their bad decisions . . . Oh, *right*.

QUEEN ELIZABETH'S "VIRGIN" COLADA

It's not easy being the most powerful person in all the land, especially when half of your subjects think they should be on top of you. Literally. But Queen Elizabeth knew how to enjoy her forty-five years as supreme monarch: by staying single. Shakespeare gives the Virgin Queen a shout-out in *A Midsummer Night's Dream* as the "fair vestal thronèd by the west" whom Cupid tries to shoot with his love arrow. And, after her death, he memorialized her virginity in *Henry VIII* by describing baby Elizabeth's eternal purity: "a most unspotted lily shall she pass / To the

PER TAL VARIAR SON QVI

MOR... ...TVA
Anno
MISERICORDIA

ELIZABETH that famous Queene lives
Who govern'd England foure and fourty
Wild Irish tam'd, Low country protected
Friended France, foyld Spaine & Pope...
Foes found her powerfull, all People vertuous
The World wise and iust Heau'n religeous
God hath her Soule, men her Admir...
ENGLAND her good deeds Reign for...

Elizabeth famously fashioned herself as the Virgin Queen and made some great speeches to Parliament about how she couldn't possibly get married: she loved her country and her subjects way too much to let anyone else—especially a foreign guy—penetrate her, um, borders. Her suitors included (but were not limited to): the Catholic horse breeder Archduke Charles of Austria, the mentally unstable King Eric of Sweden, and the French boy-toy Francis, Duke of Anjou. Behind the scenes, she may have opened her royal coffer for local favorites Christopher Hatton, Robert Dudley, and his stepson Robert Devereux. But that's for her to know, and us to never find out.

ground." Elizabeth understood that marriage would mean sharing her power. Plus, by never producing an heir she could get back at her father, Henry VIII. He obsessed about having a legitimate son and killed her mother, Anne Boleyn, when she couldn't give him one. *You want a little Mini-Me to take over the throne, Daddy? How about I end your bloodline altogether? Howdya like them apples?* Well played, Bess. Well played. We don't actually believe Elizabeth abstained all those years, so we've tossed out the cherry garnish and paired this virgin drink with a chaser of white rum.

> 3 cups crushed ice
> 1 cup fresh strawberries
> 1 cup pineapple juice
> ½ cup cream of coconut
> 2 ounces white rum (optional)
> Extra strawberry, for garnish

Fill a blender with the ice. Add the strawberries, pineapple juice, and cream of coconut. Blend until smooth. If adding rum, pour it into the blender and mix for a few more seconds. Garnish with a strawberry. Make like a minion and serve immediately.

HIPPOLYTA'S BODY SHOTS

A Midsummer Night's Dream opens with Duke Theseus telling his war prisoner/fiancée, Hippolyta, queen of the Amazons: "I wooed thee with my sword, / And won thy love doing thee injuries." Now, we may not have degrees in couples counseling, but this doesn't seem like an effec-

MINI-BARD Shakespeare would have known about the legendary Amazons from ancient writers like Herodotus, Virgil, and Pliny the Elder, and from more recent travelers' accounts. Stories about these women warriors (rumored to wander the steppes of Russia, the wilds of South America, and even California) made Englishmen quiver in their codpieces. The Amazons allegedly seared off one of their breasts to make it easier to use a bow and arrow or hold a shield. To keep up their numbers, they had sex with random men from neighboring territories once a month to get pregnant, and then kept the girl babies. The boy babies didn't fare as well: the Amazons sent a lucky few back to their dads but killed or maimed the rest. Why did English explorers like Sir Walter Raleigh perpetuate these tales—even when they'd never laid eyes on an actual Amazon? Could it be they were working through a wee bit of anxiety about serving an all-powerful Lady Boss, Elizabeth I? Hmmmm?

tive way to build a healthy foundation of trust and mutual respect. Even though Hippolyta ends up married to Theseus at the end of the play, we know she'd rather be partying with her single warrior girlfriends, whipping off her top, and moshing her man-hating self all over the dance floor. This drink lets you party like an Amazon all night long—and still stay alert enough to operate a bow and arrow.

> 1 sugar packet
> Lemon wedge
> 1 ounce vodka
> 2 ounces Mountain Dew

Lick the neck of the person closest to you. Tilt his/her head and pour the sugar packet on the wet spot. Put the lemon into his/her mouth, skin side in. Lick the sugar, shoot the vodka, suck the lemon from the other person's mouth, and follow with a shot of Mountain Dew.

❧ Savory Matters ❧

CELIA'S KALE FRIEND-CHIPS

When Rosalind gets banished from her uncle's kingdom in *As You Like It*, Celia, ever the faithful friend and cousin, runs away with her into the Forest of Arden. Celia's such a good sport, in fact, that she agrees to wear the Dumpy Poor Lady disguise while Rosalind gets to dress up as the dashing male lead *and* carry a cool boar-spear. And, like all those best friends who stand by their prettier, wittier, star-of-the-show counterparts, Celia stays loyal even after Rosalind drops her for a guy she's met only once. We'd love to tell Celia that she doesn't have to wait around for Rosalind to come back in case Orlando dumps her—and that she's definitely not obligated to date Orlando's loser brother if it *does* work out. Better to spend an evening sharing these tasty kale chips with some cool new gal pals than making unrequited friendship bracelets. They're a healthy, empowered twist on the classic Sad Ditched Friend can of Pringles. • *4 servings*

1 large bunch flat (not curly-leaved) kale
2 teaspoons olive oil
Olive oil spray
Merlot salt (or flavored salt of your choice)
Toasted sesame seeds

Preheat the oven to 300°F. Rinse the kale and dry *thoroughly*. When completely dry, cut the kale leaves off the hard stems and rip them into chip-size pieces. Discard the stems. Place the kale in a bowl and, using your hands, coat the leaves with olive oil. Spread the kale evenly on a cookie sheet and bake until the chips are crispy (20–25 minutes). Let cool. Pour the chips into a large bowl and lightly coat with olive oil spray, tossing gently to mix. Sprinkle the chips with salt, to taste, and sesame seeds.

~✥~

MISTRESS OVERDONE'S OYSTER SHOOTERS WITH SPICY STEWED TOMATOES

No Shakespeare play would be complete without a reference to whoring, fishmongers, or houses of ill repute (or "stews," as they commonly were called). The brothel-owning bawd Mistress Overdone has just a few lines, but she packs a big thematic punch in the morally hypocritical world of *Measure for Measure*. When the authorities start breathing down her neck, she fights for the right to keep her business open. We believe she speaks for all entrepreneurial single women when she complains, "Shall all our houses of resort in the suburbs be pulled down?" Right on, sister! Long live the stews!—including this tasty base for an oyster shooter.

• *24 shooters*

1 (14-ounce) can stewed tomatoes

1 tablespoon minced fresh ginger

2 cloves garlic, minced

Zest and juice of 1 lime

Juice of 1 lemon

¼ cup fresh orange juice

3 tablespoons ketchup

2 teaspoons sriracha

24 shucked oysters, removed from shells

MINI-BARD Mistress Overdone's "suburbs" refer to some pretty risqué sixteenth- and seventeenth-century London neighborhoods that were beyond the lord mayor's jurisdiction. These areas, especially Bankside where Shakespeare's Globe Theatre was, had plenty of room for playhouses, brothels, and taverns. Not exactly the family fare of today's Chuck E. Cheeses and Targets. Henry VIII and James I (who was king when Shakespeare wrote *Measure for Measure*) both tried to tear the houses down, but with little success. The brothels were called "stews" because of their associations with the steam baths clients took to sweat out the venereal diseases they picked up there. Or possibly because *stew* was a medieval word for *fishpond*, and there were a lot of them out that way. Go ahead, let the steamy/fishy/ladyparts-y puns fly. Shakespeare certainly did.

Puree the tomatoes in a food processor. Add the ginger, garlic, lime zest and juice, lemon juice, orange juice, ketchup, and sriracha, and pulse 10 times. Chill in the refrigerator for 2 hours. Fill shot glasses halfway with the tomato mixture and place 1 oyster in each. Serve immediately.

~⚜~

CRESSIDA'S GREEK TURNOVERS WITH MEDITERRANEAN PICKLE

In the Trojan War drama *Troilus and Cressida*, Pandarus pimps his niece, Cressida, out to a Trojan prince (it's where we get the verb *to pander*). Then Cressida's father trades her to the Greeks, where she winds up sleeping with Diomedes. Talk about a quick turnover. This single girl's flip-flopping between the sheets and across enemy lines earns her a reputation for willingly offering herself up as "sluttish spoils"—which is a little harsh considering her position as a pawn in her male relatives' schemes. (Too bad she didn't ditch the lot of them and join ranks with the Amazons who, according to legend, were there fighting for the Trojans.) The only bright spot for Cressida is that Shakespeare's Helen of Troy—the flirty face that launched a thousand Greek warships—comes off looking like even more of a bimbo than she does. We've brought some bite to this traditional spanakopita by adding Mediterranean pickle, since that's exactly what Cressida finds herself in.   • *60 hors d'oeuvres*

⅓ cup olive oil

2 pounds baby spinach, washed

1 bunch scallions, white and green parts chopped

continued...

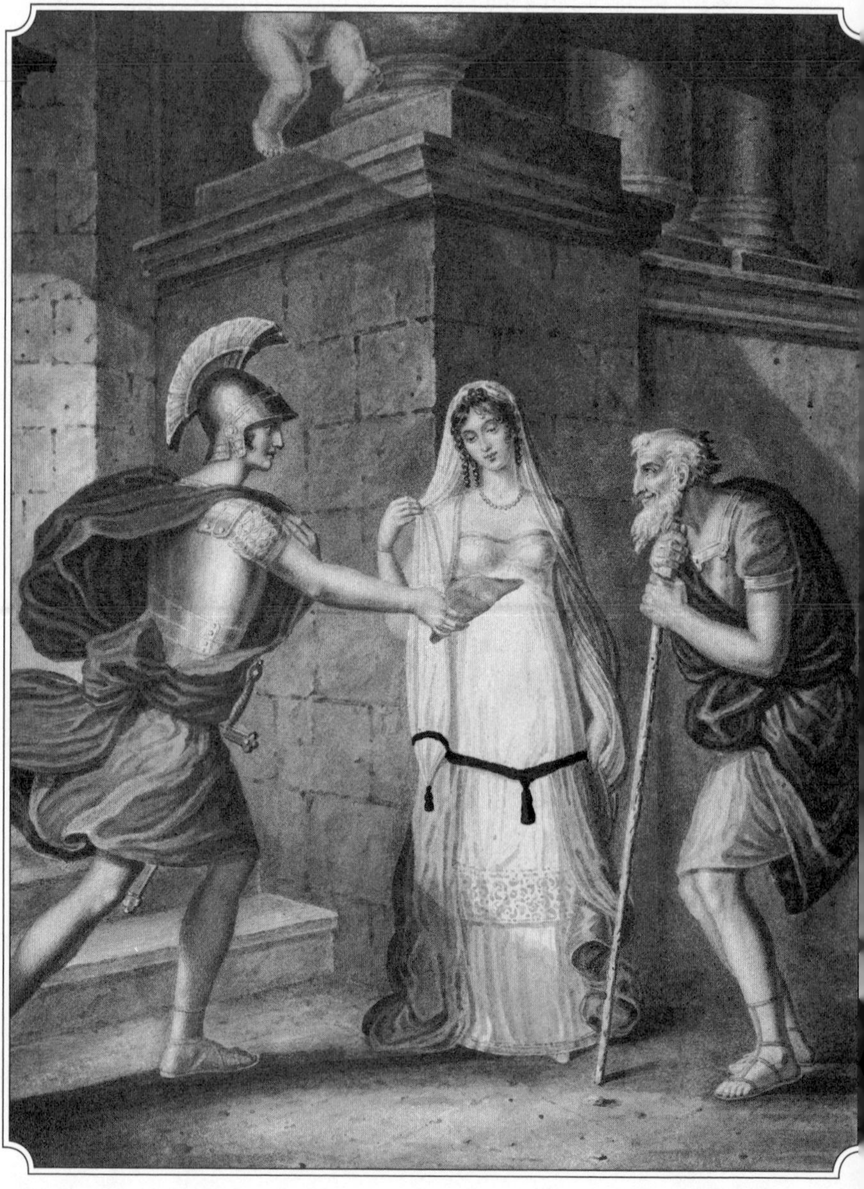

Salt and pepper

½ cup part-skim ricotta cheese

1 cup crumbled feta cheese

½ cup freshly grated Parmesan

2 eggs, lightly beaten

3 Mediterranean pickles, diced, plus more for garnish

1 pound phyllo pastry sheets

1 cup (2 sticks) butter

Sauté the spinach in 2 tablespoons oil until wilted. Remove from the pan, squeeze out the liquid, and chop. Add the remaining oil to the pan and sauté scallions for 3 minutes. Put the spinach back in the pan with the scallions and salt and pepper, to taste, and cook for 1 to 2 minutes. Remove from the pan and let cool in a bowl.

Once cool, add the ricotta, feta, Parmesan, eggs, and pickles, and mix together.

Preheat the oven to 350°F. Melt the butter in a small saucepan over low heat.

Unroll the phyllo dough and keep unused layers covered with plastic wrap and a damp towel so they don't dry out. Take one sheet and brush it with melted butter. Place another sheet on top of this one, brush with butter, and repeat with two more sheets. Cut the pile of four buttered sheets into 3-inch-wide vertical strips. Place 1–2 tablespoons of spinach filling 1 inch from the end of each strip. With each strip, fold the end over the filling to form a triangle, then continue to fold up the strip in triangles until you have one wrapped turnover. Place the filled triangles on a baking sheet, brush the tops with butter, and bake for 20 to 25 minutes, or until golden brown. Repeat with the remaining phyllo sheets and filling. Serve on a platter surrounded by pickles.

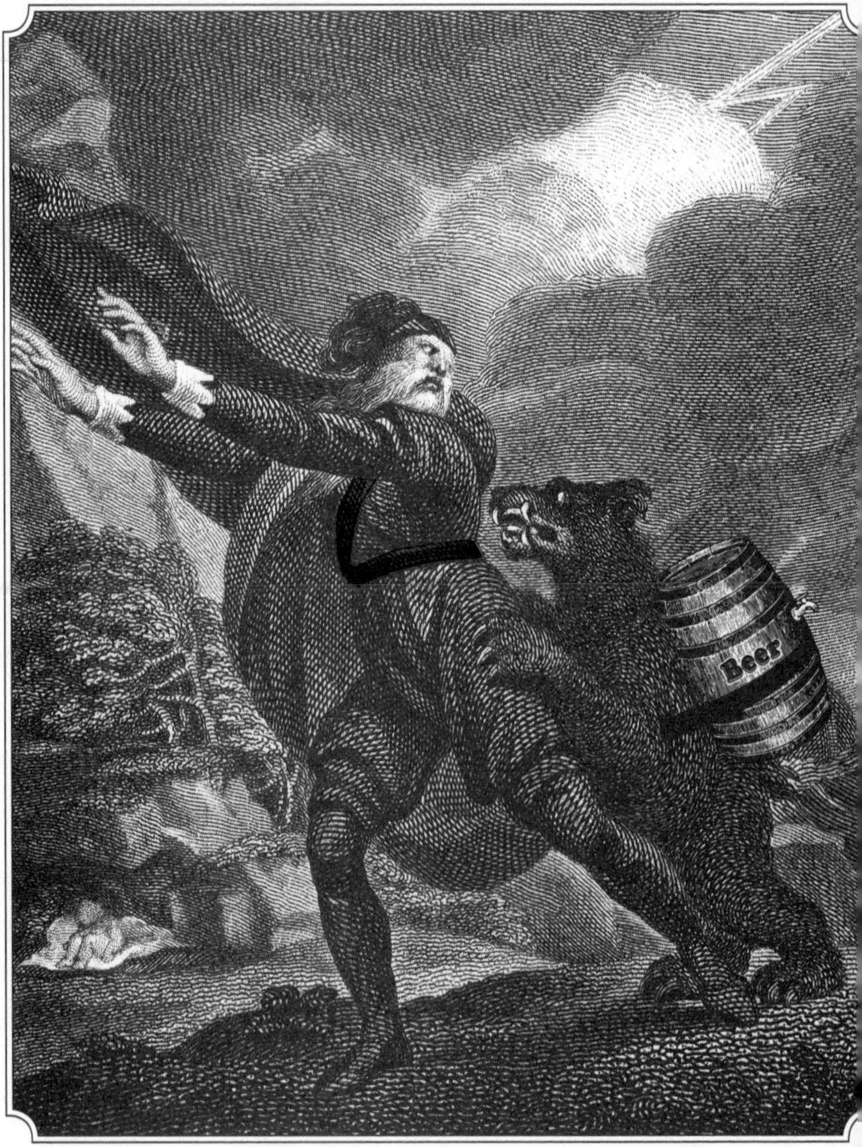
Beer

VII

Exit, Pursued by a Beer

Drowning Your Sorrows

Feeling disrespected at work? At least none of your colleagues are trying to kill you. Did your crazy ex-boyfriend crash your funeral, beat up your brother, and trash your grave site? We didn't think so. Get some perspective on your troubles by enjoying a cocktail and snack inspired by the bona fide crap lives of Shakespeare's most tragic characters—like Antigonus from *The Winter's Tale*. When he refuses to let paranoid King Leontes kill his newborn princess, Antigonus is ordered to chuck the baby into the wilderness himself. That's where he gets chased off in the most famous stage direction ever: *Exit, pursued by a bear.* And then mauled to death. While a moron clown-boy watches. Still think you've got problems? Read on. Unlike the hopeless cases here, things will definitely look better for you in the morning.

THE DROWNING OPHELIA

Like many Shakespeareans, we're curious about the sketchy circumstances of Ophelia's death by drowning in *Hamlet*. Gertrude makes it sound like an accident, but other characters consider it a suicide. There's enough suspicion around her death to deny her all the religious bells and whistles at her funeral. She does get a *semi*-holy burial, though (which Hamlet proceeds to desecrate anyway, but we digress). So many questions are left unanswered: Did she kill herself because she was heartbroken over Hamlet's douchey treatment of her? Was she so distressed about her father's murder that she lost her mind and thought her dress was a boat? Or was she just a klutz "clambering" up a tree to hang flower garlands? What was she thinking before she got sucked into the muck? (Maybe, *Damn, why did I pick the heavy beading today of all days?*) We'll never know for sure, but we think she'd appreciate this pretty blue cocktail garnished with edible flowers. It may not have saved her in the end, but it definitely would have made those last moments less of a drag.

Edible flowers
1 egg white
Dusting of sugar
1 ounce vodka
¼ ounce blue curaçao
¾ ounce St.-Germain elderflower liqueur
Juice of ½ lemon

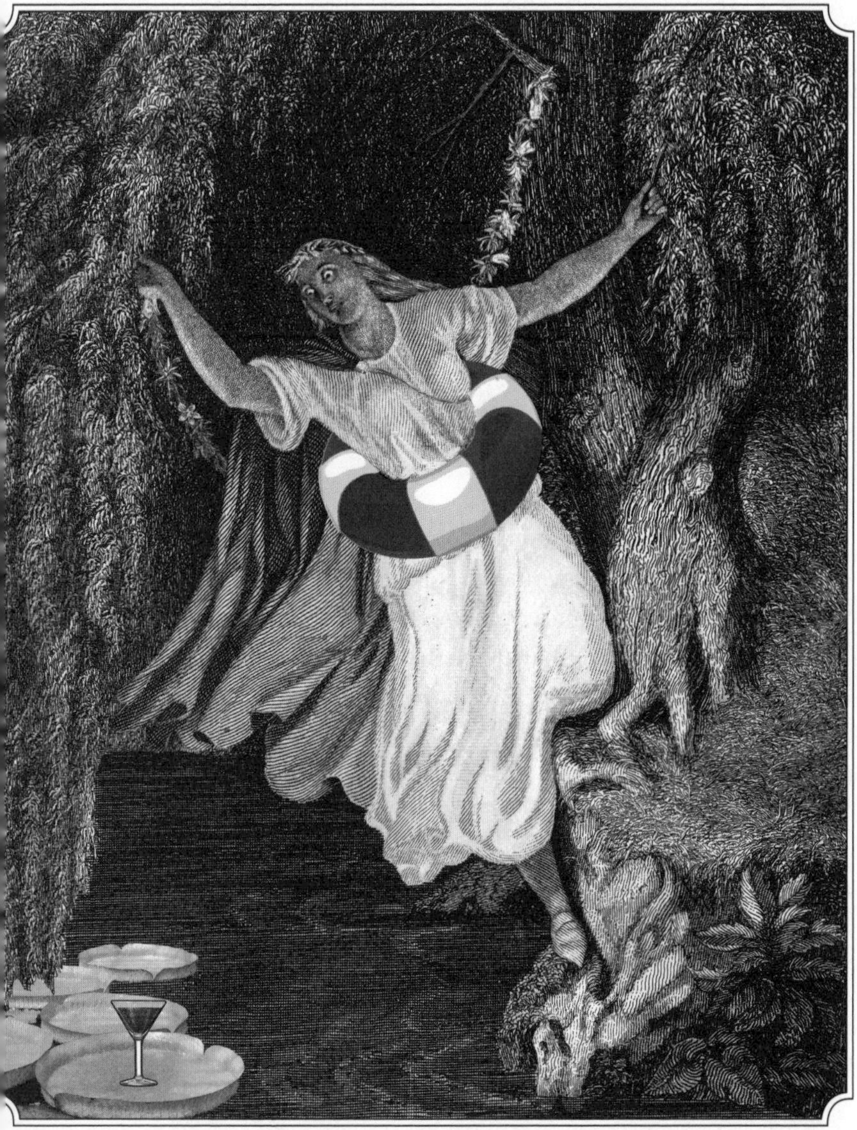

Ophelia has a lot of insightful things to say in the first three acts of *Hamlet*, but she's often just remembered as the Girl Who Drowned. According to Edgar Allan Poe, "the death . . . of a beautiful woman is unquestionably the most poetical topic in the world." This kind of thinking may explain why artists across the centuries have fixated on illustrating Ophelia's final moments, which happen offstage in the play. Most of them follow Gertrude's description of her in the "weeping brook" with "Her clothes spread wide, / And, mermaid-like." Whether it's John Everett Millais's classic circa 1852 portrait of an angelic Ophelia floating with her flowers, or Julia Stiles submerged in a Manhattan fountain surrounded by Ethan "Hamlet" Hawke's love letters, "Drowning Ophelia" is an icon not of an age but for all time.

Prepare the edible flowers beforehand by lightly brushing the flowers with egg white. Dust with sugar, shaking off any excess. Allow to dry. Shake all the liquid ingredients together with ice. Strain and pour into a martini glass. Garnish with the flowers.

"ET TU, BRUT"
CHAMPAGNE COCKTAIL

Everyone knows what it's like to have a coworker you can't trust. Maybe it's Brad, the guy who took credit for your marketing idea; or Brianne, the head of Human Resources who keeps "losing" your performance reports. But let's be honest for a second. Have they ever tried to jump you in the cafeteria? Julius Caesar thought that Brutus and Cassius were his allies, or at least his functional colleagues. He never dreamed that they'd stab him in the back. Even when he's lying on the grounds of the Capitol bleeding out, he still can't believe it: "Et tu, Bruté?"—and *you*, Brutus? We designed this cocktail to complement Caesar's doozy of a workplace betrayal. Brut champagne, like Brutus himself, is much less sweet than you'd expect.

> 1 ounce fresh blood orange juice
> Brut champagne
> Slice of blood orange

Pour the orange juice into a cocktail flute. Fill to the top with brut champagne. Garnish with an ominous slice of blood (orange). Watch your back.

~~⚔~~

OTHELLO'S GREEN-EYED MONSTER

You've made it to the top of your profession, and shown everyone that you're the best, most qualified person for the job. Like you, *Othello*'s eponymous general knows how great that feels. At the start of the play, he's head of the Venetian military and newly wedded to the young and beautiful Desdemona. But Othello had to overcome major obstacles like racism, ageism, and charges of voodoo-ism to get there. As the play unfolds, the malicious Iago preys on "black" Othello's vulnerable associations with Africa and Islam to make the Moor doubt that his white, Christian wife and employers would ever stay faithful to an outsider like him. Once Iago stirs up that "green-eyed monster" of jealousy, Othello spends the rest of the play spiraling into a paranoid, violent rage. Perhaps old insecurities gnaw at *you*, too. Why weren't you invited to the CEO's Christmas party? And what's with that gossipy guy in Sales who's always trying to mess with your head? *As if your wife would be seen dead at Panera with Gary, your trusted VP. That's ridiculous! She doesn't even eat carbs.* Take a cue from the doomed Moor of Venice, and stop that jealous monster in its tracks. Better yet, drink it down. You'll feel much, much better.

1½ ounces Midori melon liqueur

1 ounce vodka

2 ounces fresh orange juice

1 ounce simple syrup

Juice of ½ lime

Juice of ½ lemon

2 small, scooped honeydew melon balls, for garnish

Shake the liquid ingredients together with ice and strain into a martini glass. Add melon balls for a "green-eyed" garnish.

MINI-BARD From his appearance on the play's title page as "the Moor of Venice" to his final lines, Othello is a man defined by his cultural outsider status. Although a Moor was technically someone from the Barbary coast of Africa, it was a term that Shakespeare's audiences would have associated with all kinds of non-Christian and/or non-fair-skinned foreigners, especially Muslims, Turks, and Arabs. Oh—and also the Devil. Even though Othello is a converted Moor, and claims to come from men of royal stock, he just can't shake the feeling that he isn't as good as the noble, white, Christian-born Venetians he works for. In his final speech, Othello recalls fighting for Venice against "a malignant and a turbaned Turk." As he describes how he "took by th' throat the circumcisèd dog / And smote him," he turns the blade against himself. Shakespeare may not have known the term "internalized racism," but this is one brutal and brilliant commentary on it.

ten

THAISA'S MUDSLIDE

Ophelia may be the most famous Shakespearean heroine to end up dead in the water, but she certainly isn't the last. And at least she gets a half-way decent burial. Thaisa, from *Pericles*, should be so lucky. She dies giving birth to her daughter on a ship in the middle of a tempest, then gets tossed overboard by the superstitious deckhands who think her corpse is causing the storm. Her husband, Pericles, agrees that they should cast her, "scarcely coffined, in the ooze." (In other words, dump her into the mud, nailed inside a box they found lying around below deck.) But, guess what? She's *not* dead. And she's not David Blaine. She's just in some kind of pseudo-dead state. When Thaisa washes up on the shores of Ephesus, she's revived by a physician, and then—convinced that everyone she loves is gone—cloisters herself in the Temple of Diana for fourteen years. We wish we could have given her a pitcher of these mudslides to erase the memory of that first disastrous one.

> 1½ ounces vodka
> ¾ ounce Kahlúa
> ¾ ounce Amarula
> KitKat bar

Pour the liquid ingredients into a short glass over ice. Add a KitKat segment as an edible stirrer to re-create Thaisa's makeshift casket.

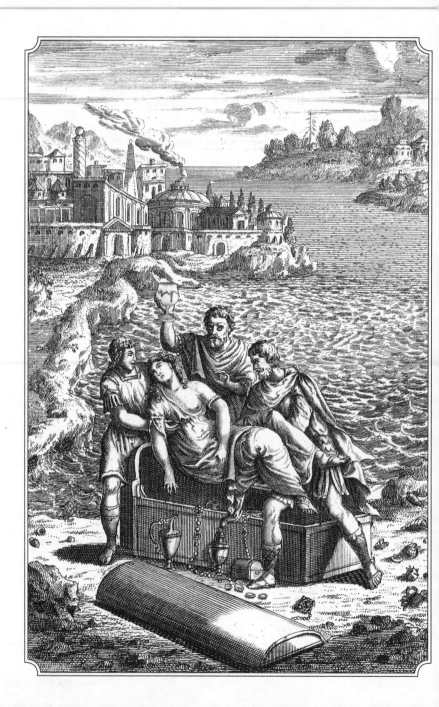

⟶ SAVORY MATTERS ⟵

DESDEMONA'S DIVIDED MOZZARELLA

It's hard to find any touching "father of the bride" moments in Shake-speare's plays: daughters are usually punished for choosing the men they love over the men who raised them. *Cymbeline*'s Imogen gets exiled by her father for marrying Posthumus against his will. And King Lear ban-ishes Cordelia for stating the obvious: it would be *super creepy* to love your father more than your husband. But *Othello*'s Desdemona suffers the most for what she calls her "divided duty." After her father, Braban-tio, disowns her for eloping with Othello, Desdemona devotes herself to standing by her man, even when it means leaving her native country and following him to war. Hey, Othello, how about some nice diamond earrings to show your appreciation? A charm for her Pandora bracelet? A *card*? Sadly, none of these "thanks for always being there" gifts are in Desdemona's future. Instead, Othello buys into the evil Iago's logic: if Desdemona deceived her father, surely she would deceive her husband, too. This isn't going to end well. (See Iago's Con-i-kaze, page 57.) But, lucky for you, the only "divided duty" here involves halving some moz-zarella balls and cherry tomatoes.   • *20 hors d'oeuvres*

⅓ cup olive oil

2 tablespoons balsamic vinegar

20 fresh mozzarella balls, halved

20 cherry tomatoes, halved

1 large bunch basil, washed and dried

Toothpicks

½ cup pine nuts, lightly toasted

In a bowl, mix the oil and vinegar. Add the mozzarella balls to the bowl, coating them evenly with the mixture. Cover and refrigerate for at least 2 hours. Assemble 20 toothpick skewers in layers of cheese, basil leaf, tomato. Arrange on a plate and sprinkle with pine nuts.

<hr />

ROSENCRANTZ AND GUILDENSTERN'S BROWN-NOSER STEAK BITES

Congratulations! You finally got invited to the royal castle! You've been putting up with your childhood buddy Hamlet's pompous existential ramblings for years—and, at last, it's paid off! What's next? A ski vacation at the royal resort in Lillehammer? An invite to the Cannes Juggling Festival on the family's private jet? *Uh-oh. Slow down there, boys.* The only reason you're on that cruise to England with Hamlet is because King Claudius wants you to help get his stepson executed. You're supposed to deliver a letter to the English king that says, "Kill Hamlet when you get this," but Hamlet's going to find it while you're snoozing in the guest cabin. And guess who's in his rewrite? Yep. Just when you thought all that ass-kissing had paid off, Hamlet goes and gets *you* executed. This one's for all you failed brown-nosers out there. No one can say you didn't try.   • *45–50 hors d'oeuvres*

> 8 ounces amber ale
>
> 2 cloves garlic, peeled and crushed
>
> 1 (2-ounce) tin anchovies, liquid and fillets
>
> 1 tablespoon brown sugar
>
> Salt and pepper
>
> 1½ pounds steak tips

1 large bulb fennel, cored and thinly sliced, fronds reserved

Thin slices of baguette

Olive oil

Whole-grain mustard

Combine the ale, garlic, anchovies, sugar, and salt and pepper, to taste, in a shallow dish. Marinate the steak in the mixture overnight. Grill the steak until medium-rare. Cut into thin slices. Grill the fennel. Brush thin slices of baguette with olive oil and place under the broiler to toast. Spread some mustard on each piece of baguette and top with a piece of fennel and then steak. Top with chopped fennel fronds and more pepper, to taste. Make sure that the most powerful people in the room get first dibs.

~❖~

MALVOLIO'S DEVILED LEGGS

No one suffers a more public and prolonged humiliation than the priggish servant Malvolio in *Twelfth Night*. What begins as a bit of fun at his expense spirals into some hard-core bullying worthy of an *ABC Afterschool Special*. The partying Sir Toby Belch and his sidekick Maria devise a plan to make Malvolio think that his boss, Countess Olivia, loves him. Maria forges a letter from Olivia instructing him to wear yellow stockings with crossed garters and to smile all the time if he wants to please her. The love-struck Malvolio obliges, and makes a total fool of himself in front of Olivia, who actually hates yellow stockings with crossed garters. And smiling. All of his erratic behavior makes it easy for his tormentors to continue with their "sportful malice," charging him with insanity, locking him in a dark room, and call-

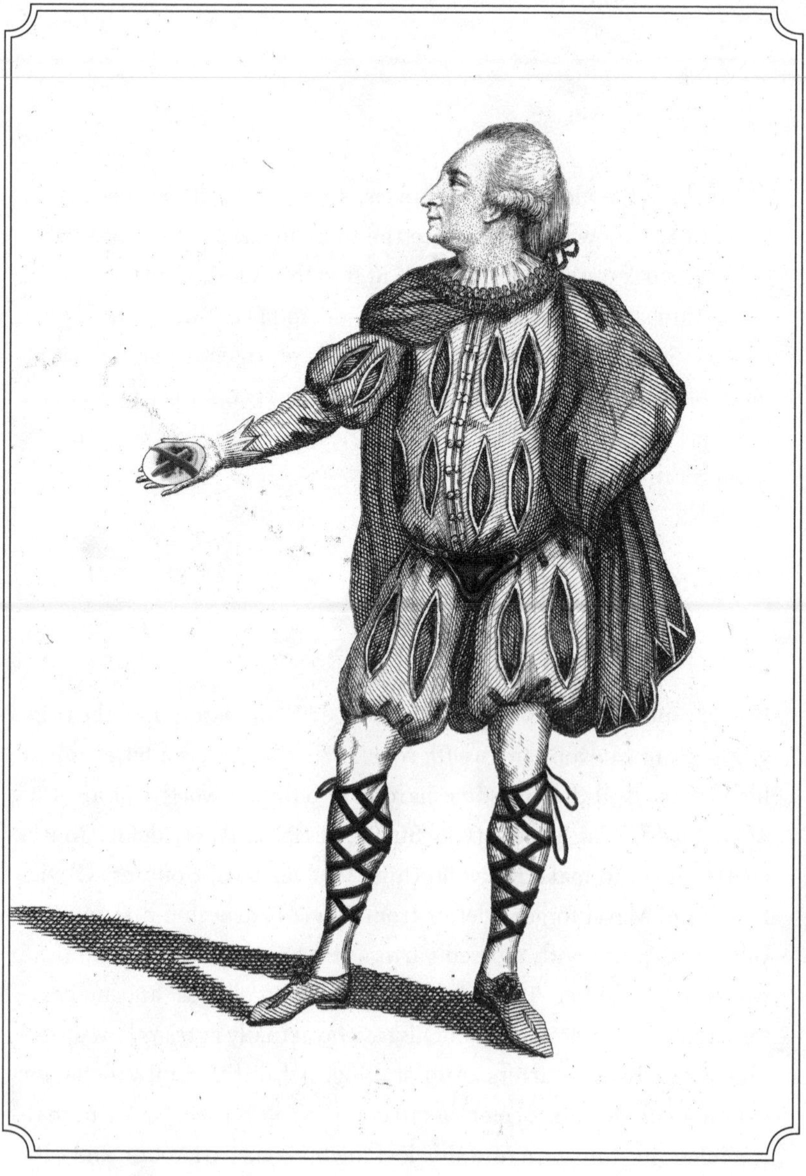

ing him a devil. Malvolio's demonized for his yellow stockings, but our Deviled Leggs will make you the most popular host in town. And then you can take revenge on whomever you want by leaving them off the guest list.

• *24 hors d'oeuvres*

12 large eggs
1 teaspoon whole-grain mustard
½ cup mayonnaise
2 teaspoons rice vinegar
Roasted red peppers, cut into thin strips

Place the eggs in a pan with water just covering them and bring to a boil. Remove from the heat, cover, and let sit for 12 minutes. Place in the

MINI-BARD   As Malvolio finds out the hard way, when you try to accessorize your way up the social ladder, you may have a long, painful fall. Especially when you're a steward with dreams of becoming a Count and wearing a "branched velvet gown" embroidered with a fancy tree motif. During the sixteenth century, sumptuary laws limited what kinds of cloth and colors you could wear depending on your social class. The laws became more strict over the course of the century, partially in reaction to a growing middle-class population with expendable income who could buy the same fancy clothes as their higher-ups. It was getting harder and harder to tell old-moneyed blue bloods from new-moneyed citizens. You could dress down (like Viola does when she suits up as Cesario to serve Duke Orsino), but you couldn't dress up.

fridge until well cooled. Peel the eggs. Halve them lengthwise and re-move the yolks. In a bowl, mash the yolks together with mustard, may-onnaise, and vinegar. Fill each white with a spoonful of yolk mixture. Cross 2 red pepper strips across each yolk to create a "cross-gartered" effect. Arrange on a platter and serve.

VIII

Lend Me Your Cheers

Party Like It's 1599!

In our day, as in Shakespeare's, when life throws you lemons, you might make some very tasty limoncello. Shakespeare did just that when he turned life's trials and tribulations into a positive community experience. People from all walks of life came to the playhouse to see his works performed, and (when it wasn't plague season) they left those two to three smelly, entertaining hours of fellowship in high spirits. He loved to pun on how his Globe Theatre was a smaller version of the globe we stand and stumble on together every day. Like Mark Antony's rousing eulogy in *Julius Caesar*—which begins with a call for his countrymen to "lend me your ears"—great speeches can unite their listeners in profound and moving ways. We've created these drinks and hors d'oeuvres to honor Shakespeare's embrace of our big, beautiful, messy human condition. They're inspired by the special events and celebrations that we share with each other. But feel free to enjoy them whenever the spirits move you. Cheers!

CALIBAN'S WRONG ISLAND ICED TEA

Spiked with three kinds of booze, this concoction is our tribute to Caliban, the native Prospero enslaves after he washes up on the shores of Caliban's island in *The Tempest*. If Caliban had known how to speak Prospero's language from the get-go, he could have told him: *You've messed with the wrong island, signor*. Instead, Caliban loses everything to a usurping Italian who calls him a "born devil." Eventually, Caliban *does* learn how to curse from the play's intrusive colonizers—and how to drink, when a few more shipwrecked Europeans show up. Let our tropical version of the classic Long Island iced tea help you take back total cocktail domination at your next beach party. And we do mean *your* beach.

> 1 ounce Laird's Applejack
> ½ ounce vodka
> ½ ounce Gosling's dark Bermuda rum
> ½ ounce sour mix
> 2 ounces pineapple juice
> Fresh pineapple wedges, for garnish

Mix all the liquid ingredients together in a highball glass. Fill to the top with crushed ice. Garnish with a pineapple wedge. Don't share with anyone, even if they offer you cool stuff for it.

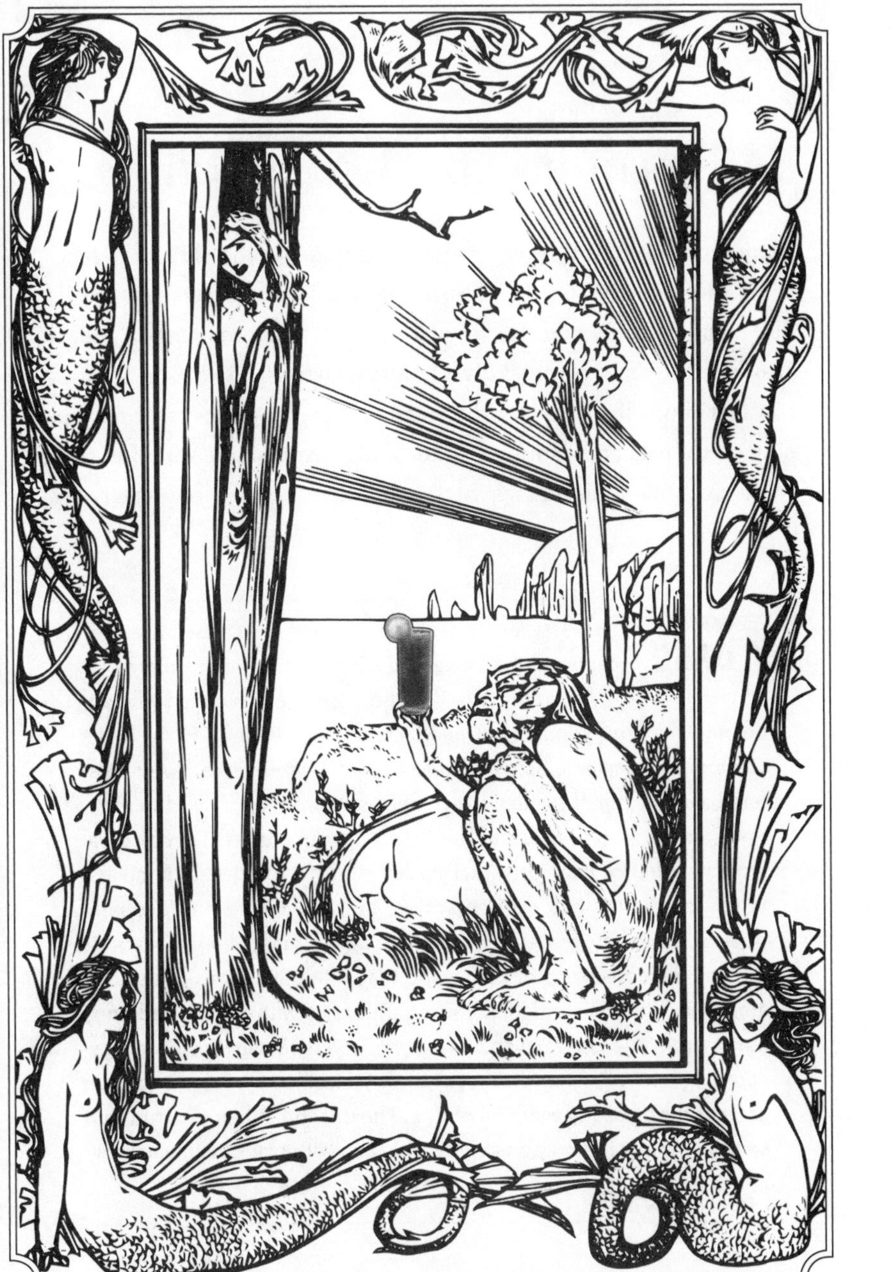

THE WEIRD SISTERS'
BLOOD AND HAND PUNCH

"Something wicked this way comes"—right down the old hatch! *Macbeth*'s cauldron-stirring Weird Sisters would love to brew a vat of this Blood and Hand Punch and serve it up at a Halloween party. (They'd also love to come to your kids' birthday parties and christenings, so consider yourself warned.) If the witches' everyday antics involve chopping off thumbs and damning infant souls, just imagine what fun they could conjure on this official witch holiday!   • *13 servings*

MINI-BARD Shakespeare went whole hag when he created his three chappy-lipped, bearded witches. They're definitely a far cry from the trio of well-dressed gentlewomen who appear in his primary source for the Macbeth story, Raphael Holinshed's *Chronicles of England, Scotland, and Ireland*. Shakespeare's Weird Sisters have a distinctly wilder streak: they summon severe weather systems, cruise around in sieves, and steal human organs. They also pal around with their demon animal guides, otherwise known as familiars. Witch-lore varied between countries, but in England and Scotland popular belief held that they had hidden devil's marks—extra teats for nursing their creepy spirit-kitties and toads. But Shakespeare's sisters aren't just freakish cat ladies mixing up brews with unbaptized body parts. From the Old English word *wyrd*, or *fate*, Macbeth's prophecy-spouting "weird" sisters also recall the mythical female Fates who spun and cut the thread of every man's life. The upshot? When they run with scissors, *you're* the only one who's going to get hurt. Cue up cackling: *Ah-ha-ha-ha-ha!*

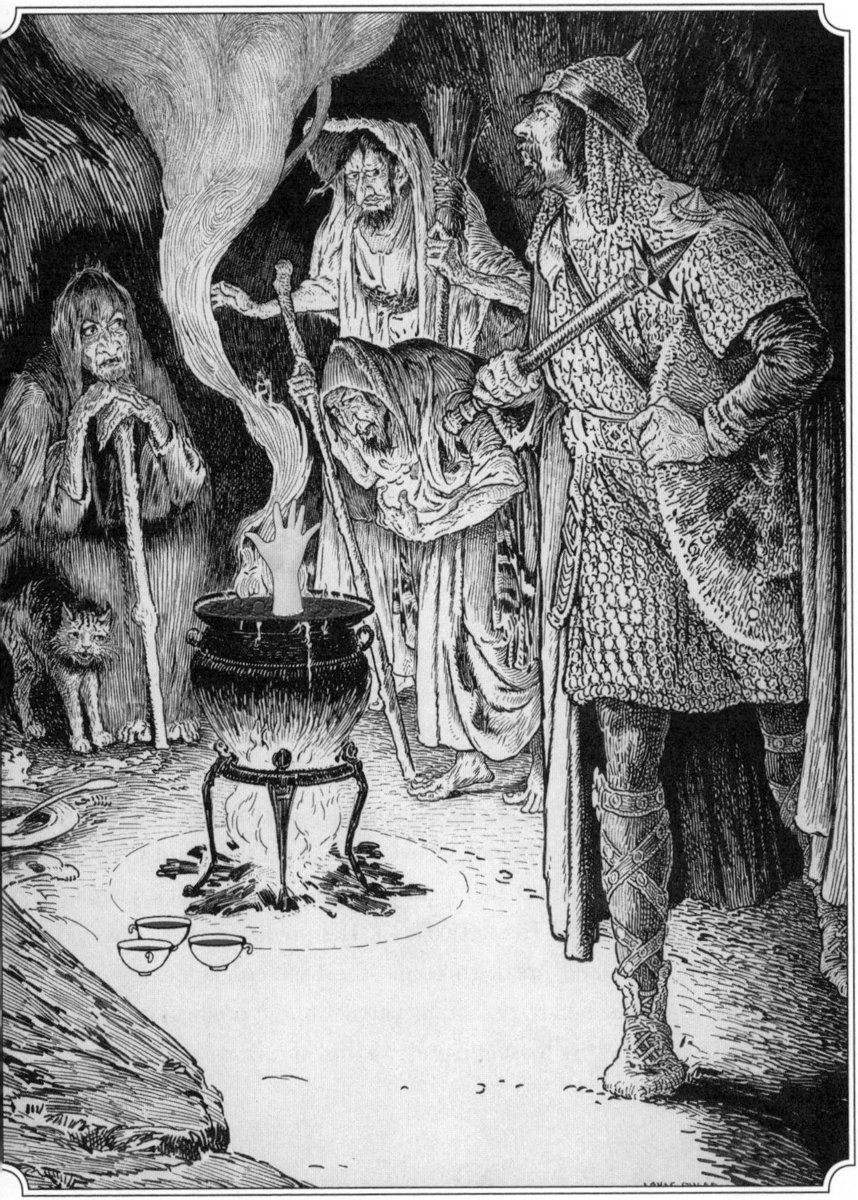

2 surgical gloves and string

13 ounces blended Scotch whisky

13 ounces vermouth rosso

13 ounces Heering cherry liqueur

13 ounces fresh orange juice

Using surgical gloves as a mold, fill them with water and tie off at the wrist with string. Freeze, then peel off the gloves to create ice hands. (You can also make ice thumbs by filling just that digit of each glove with water and tying off at its base.) Mix the drink ingredients together in a punch bowl and float the hands or thumbs on top.

~⚜~

PRINCE HAL'S TEQUILA SON-RISE

So the late bloomer's finally graduating. Congratulations! Prince Hal took *his* sweet time, too. For a while there, it was looking like Henry IV's son was never going to make it to "king" in one piece. All of that hard partying at the Boar's Head Tavern with riffraff like Falstaff was a downright embarrassment to the family. Who would have thought he'd rise up in *Henry V* to invade Normandy, deliver that incredible Saint Crispin's Day speech, *and* get a hot French princess to marry him? Back when he was still slumming it in *Henry IV, Part 1*, Hal predicted that he would "imitate the sun" and break through "the base contagious clouds." Whether you're the buddy, parent, or partner of the prodigal graduate, make a Tequila Son-rise toast and pretend that *you* always knew this day would come, too.

1½ ounces tequila

1 bottle hard lemonade

½ ounce cassis liqueur

Pour the tequila into a highball glass and fill halfway with ice. Fill almost to the top with hard lemonade. Tip the glass slightly and slowly pour in the cassis at the lowered edge to create a layered sunrise effect.

⚘

KING LEAR'S
RETIRED-BUT-NOT-FORGOTTEN

Retirement is a bittersweet event. Just ask King Lear. After making a big deal about passing his kingdom on to his kids, he refuses to give up any of his royal perks. He says he wants to "unburdened crawl toward death," but what he really means is: *I am a big baby. Change my diapers and host expensive parties for me and my friends at your castles.* Okay, so maybe he didn't make the most graceful exit from his corner office, but, at the end of the day, he just didn't want to be forgotten. After all, he's only human. Whatever your retirement scenario may be, throw a party and celebrate with this bitter cynar (an artichoke liqueur) and sweet prosecco cocktail.

Lemon rind spiral

1 ounce cynar

4 ounces prosecco

3 ounces club soda

Make a lemon rind spiral and place in the freezer. (This will produce a prolonged, celebratory fizz when placed in the drink.) In a champagne

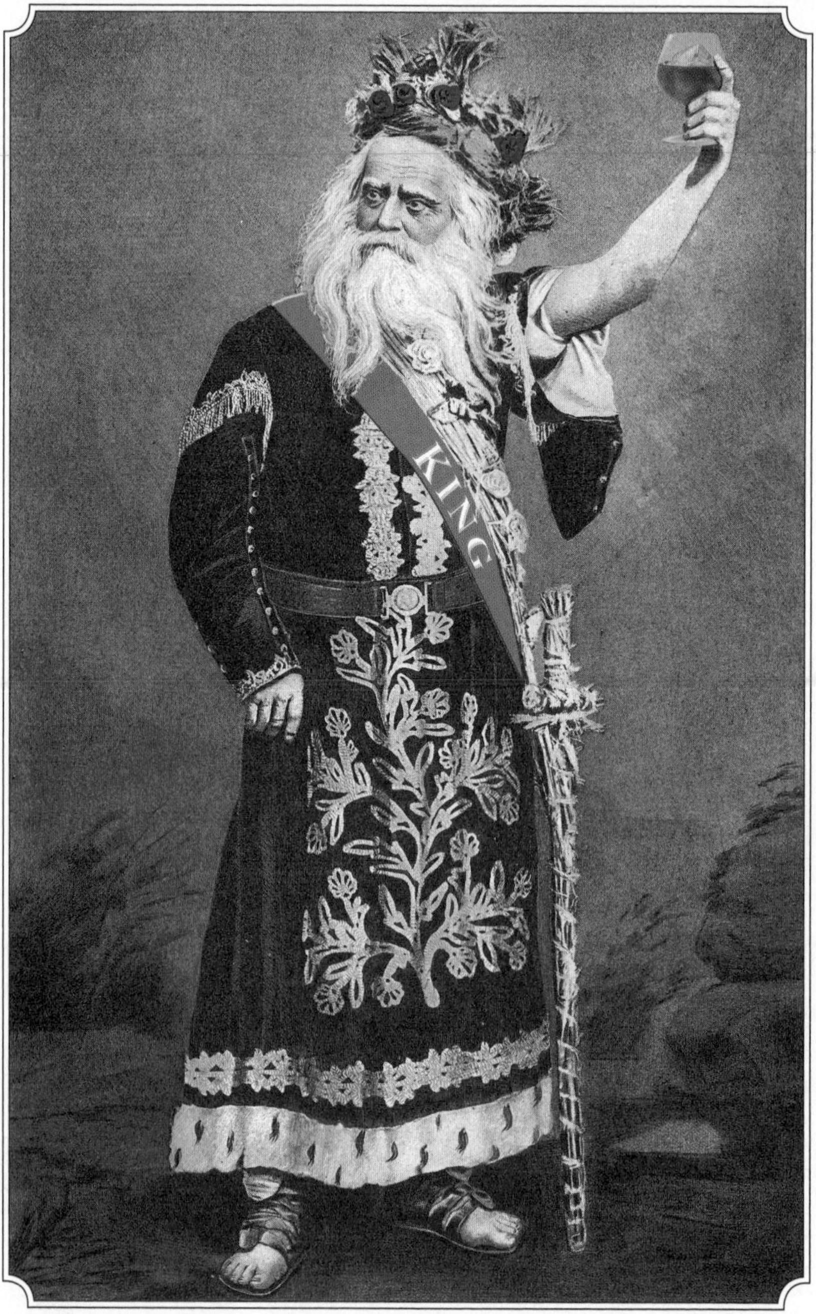
KING

flute, stir together the cynar and prosecco. Top off with the club soda. Place the spiral in the flute. Make your guests give competitive speeches about how they love you and this drink more than anyone or anything in the world.

CLEOPATRA'S "JOY OF THE WORM" BACHELORETTE SHOTS

Like Zsa Zsa Gabor, Cleopatra was an eternal optimist when it came to love and marriage. Even when she's planning her own death by snakebite at the end of *Antony and Cleopatra*, she's thinking about reuniting with her lover Antony in the afterlife: "Husband, I come"! These shots of tequila with gummy worms are inspired by the poisonous asps Cleopatra accepts from a clown who wishes her "joy of the worm" before leaving her to her fatal mission. You'll definitely want to serve up these shots at your next bachelorette party—whether it's your first or your ninth!

Gummy worm
1 ounce tequila
Salt
Lime wedge

Place a gummy worm in a shot glass and fill with tequila. Lick the back of your hand and sprinkle it with salt. To do a shot, lick the salt off your hand, down the tequila, and suck on the lime wedge. As your final act, apply worm to tongue and chew.

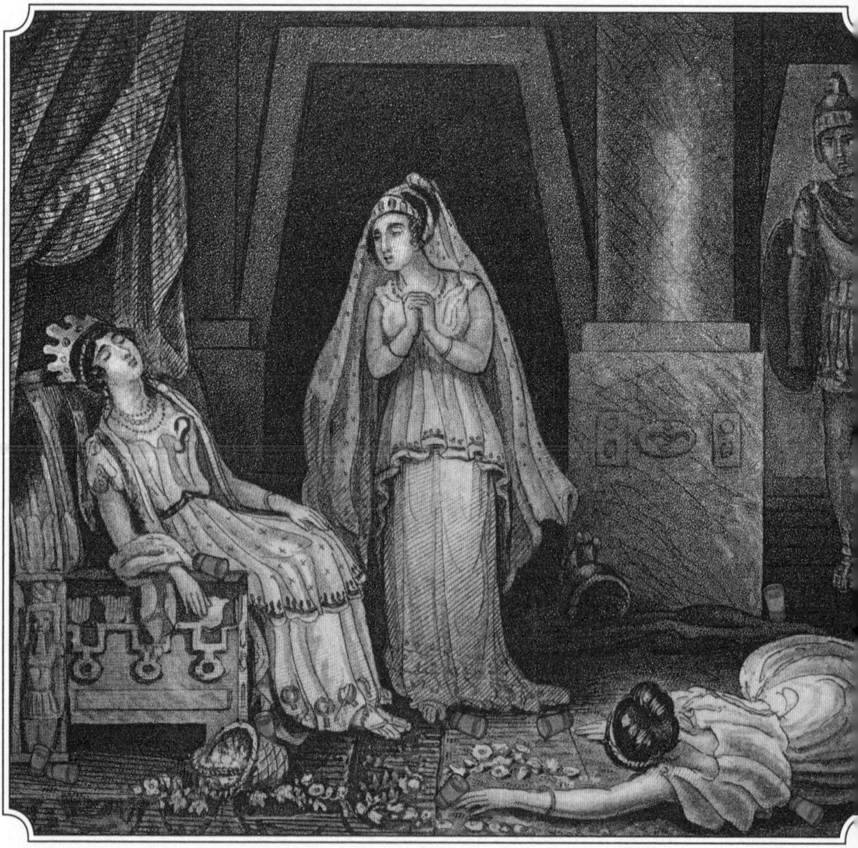

STARVELING'S MOONSHINE

Robin Starveling faced a lot of challenges playing "Moonshine" in *A Tedious Brief Scene of Young Pyramus and His Love Thisbe*. First there was his scene-stealing ass of a cast mate, Bottom. Then there were all those awkward props he had to haul around and explain to everyone—like a thorn bush, a lantern, and a dog. Not to mention that snobby audience who kept making fun of his *one freaking line*. But as any actor knows, it's not about the size of the role or the reviews, it's about the creative pro-

MINI-BARD Starveling and his crew's slapdash performance scene in *A Midsummer Night's Dream* likely recalled Shakespeare's own experiences as an actor and writer in his theater troupe. The demand for new material was high, rehearsal periods short, and the core of adult male actors supplemented by a motley crew: apprenticed boy-actors (cast in the young female parts until their voices cracked) and temporary hired hands who played the smaller roles and the musical instruments. Like Starveling's working-class gang of "rude mechanicals"—tinkers, tailors, and bellows makers—actors were low on the social totem pole. You could get rich if you had a stake in a successful company, though, as Shakespeare did as a member of the Lord Chamberlain's Men. Formed in 1594, it was the most popular troupe in London and received more invitations to perform for the royal court than any of its competitors. By 1599, they had moved to the newly built outdoor Globe Theatre, where they didn't have to pay 50 percent of their proceeds to a landlord. As a shareholder in the Globe venture, Shakespeare added some serious coin to his already well-lined purse. In other words, he wasn't just an artsy guy with a quill and a dream.

cess. What better way to celebrate than with a blowout cast party? After a couple of these Moonshine cocktails, you'll remember your one-night-only theatrical flop as the Best Experience Ever. And your fellow players as the Most Incredible, Talented People you've ever worked with.

> 1½ ounces white corn whiskey
> 1 ounce ginger liqueur
> ½ ounce simple syrup
> 1 ounce fresh lemon juice

Pour all ingredients into a shaker filled with ice. Shake while chanting "Ma-ma-ma-ma, mi-mi-mi-mi, mo-mo-mo-mo, mu-mu-mu-mu," and pour into a tall glass. Fill with ice. Back-rub circle optional.

KING JAMES'S ABSOLUT MONARCH

Promotions are always political, but some of them more so than others. Just ask James VI of Scotland. It was a rocky road down from Edinburgh to London for the man who nabbed the English throne after Elizabeth I's death in 1603. Since she had no children, the succession was hotly debated: Should the title go to the closest blood relation if it meant crowning a Scottish foreigner? Or was it better to stick with an English-born candidate, like James's cousin Lady Arbella Stuart? James ultimately got the job, but that didn't mean everyone was rushing out to buy haggis crumpets and "King James Is My Homeboy" T-shirts. Many scholars consider *Macbeth* a much-needed bit of PR for England's new king: the play showcases James's noble Scottish ancestry and forecasts

MINI-BARD When the Stuart king James VI became king of England in 1603, he took over as the patron of Shakespeare's theater group and renamed them the King's Men. This is probably why Shakespeare's company chose to mount *Macbeth* a few years later with its flattering portrayal of James's Scottish ancestor, Banquo. In the play, the witches tell Macbeth that he'll be king, but they tell Banquo that *he*'ll be the *father* of kings. Jealous Macbeth hates having a "barren sceptre" that will stop with him, so he tries to have Banquo and his son, Fleance, murdered. Fleance escapes, and in act 4, his father's ghost joins with the witches to show Macbeth a vision of Banquo's royal descendants. This line of eight Stuart kings ends with a James-like figure who holds a mirror full of future monarchs doublefisting Scottish and English sceptres. But James was actually the *ninth* Stuart monarch. Turns out, Shakespeare left out James's mother, Mary, Queen of Scots—which, given her extensive rap sheet, probably would have pleased the image-conscious James quite a bit. In 1567, Mary was forced to abdicate the Scottish throne after being accused of adultery and spousal murder. A year later, she began an eighteen-and-a-half-year stretch of imprisonment in various English castles, as Queen Elizabeth tried to keep Mary, her first cousin once removed, from killing her and taking her throne. Mary was finally executed in 1587 for allegedly conspiring to do just that. And you thought it was embarrassing when your mom wore leather pants to your high school graduation.

his union of the Scottish and English thrones. Offstage, James himself was working hard to build his brand. He cast himself as an absolute monarch, subject only to God. He also promoted the political theory of the Divine Right of kings. This meant that he was God's rep on earth, and no one could depose him—no matter how tyrannical, kilt wearing, or incompetent he was. This cocktail merges Scotch liquor and English tea into one potent Absolut combo. It's the perfect way to celebrate your contested promotion with everyone. Even if they don't like you, it's not like they have a choice.

> 1 ounce Absolut Wild Tea vodka
> ⅓ ounce Scotch whisky (preferably Chivas Regal)
> ⅓ ounce St.-Germain elderflower liqueur
> ⅓ ounce fresh lemon juice
> Crystallized ginger slice, for garnish

Pour the vodka, Scotch, St.-Germain, and lemon juice into a lowball glass over ice and stir. Garnish with ginger on a toothpick.

～✧～

JAQUES'S "7 AND 7" BIRTHDAY COCKTAIL

Jaques in *As You Like It* paints a pretty bleak picture of human existence when he delivers his Seven Ages of Man speech: "All the world's a stage, / And all the men and women merely players," stumbling through the same predictable series of roles—none of which seem very fun. But why not look on the upside of getting older and celebrate each year that you've earned? You've probably passed Jaques's first two ages: the puking infant and whining schoolboy. Perhaps you've even made it through the next two: the sighing lover and striving workaholic. Or maybe you're in the sweet spot of age #5: the wise judge. Sure, that involves a bit of a "round belly," but a discriminating taste can fill it with more sophisticated libations than 7UP. Or maybe you've already retired into the bifocaled, slipper-wearing age #6 of the "shrunk shank." Good for you! You have even *more* free time to appreciate the finer things in life. Hell, even if you're teetering on the edge of age #7, waiting to take your final curtain call, "sans teeth, sans eyes, sans taste, sans everything," you can still get a buzz on. Happy birthday!

Lime, for "party streamers" garnish
2 ounces Seagram's 7
¼ cup Rose's lime juice
2 tablespoons simple syrup
Splash of seltzer

Roll the lime on a hard surface for a minute to soften the rind. Position a citrus peeler at the top of the lime and, pressing down firmly, rotate the lime slowly to create one long "streamer." Twist it into a ringlet. Pour the Seagram's, lime juice, and simple syrup into a lowball glass over ice and stir. Top with seltzer. Dangle the rind streamer festively on rim.

SAVORY MATTERS

CRUDITÉ OF ERRORS

In Shakespeare's early slapstick *The Comedy of Errors*, Egeon's twin sons and their twin servants run around Ephesus getting mistaken for each other by spouses, prostitutes, and goldsmiths. Hilarity ensues. Decades earlier, a tempest had split Egeon's household in half, leaving his wife, one infant son, and one slave floating away. Happily, the play reunites them all in a series of unlikely events. Shakespeare's relying on some pretty outdated comic forms at this point in his career. He took most of his plot, characters, and gimmicks from the ancient Roman playwright Plautus. But, hey, he was just getting started. We're happy to cut him some slack—and some vegetables—in honor of his early experiment in comedy. These easy-to-make twin dips (to be served with the crudités of your choice) match this twins-themed play. The recipes may be simple, but they'll be crowd-pleasers. It's a perfect way to celebrate your first big professional venture—even if it does go straight to video.   • *4 cups*

DIP #1

2 cups plain, low-fat Greek yogurt

1 cup chopped dill

2 cloves garlic, peeled and crushed

1 teaspoon anchovy paste

2 tablespoons fresh lemon juice

Paprika

Mix together the yogurt, dill, garlic, anchovy paste, and lemon juice. Top with a sprinkle of paprika.

DIP #2

2 cups plain, low-fat Greek yogurt

1⅓ cups shelled pistachios

2 tablespoons fresh lemon juice

Salt

Paprika

Blend the yogurt, pistachios, lemon juice, and salt, to taste, in a food processor. If you are not at a stage in your career where you can afford a food processor, use any other means to mash the ingredients together. Serve in a bowl and top with a sprinkle of paprika.

MISTRESS QUICKLY'S POKER NIGHT CHILI

Mistress Quickly's "easy-yielding spirit" makes her Shakespeare's favorite hostess with the mostest in *Henry IV, Parts 1* and *2*, and in *Henry V*. Her Boar's Head Tavern is the first-choice gathering place for men who want to have a beer and plan drunken get-rich-quick schemes. We know they'd love her to serve up this big vat of chili when she hosts the next Eastcheap Poker Night. • *15–18 servings*

1 tablespoon olive oil

3 medium onions, diced

3 pounds ground turkey

3 (15-ounce) cans each black beans, chickpeas, and kidney beans, drained

3 (28-ounce) cans crushed tomatoes

30 ounces chicken broth

1 tablespoon ground cumin

1 tablespoon ground cinnamon

3 tablespoons kosher salt

1 teaspoon cayenne

Cook the onions in the oil over medium heat for 3 to 5 minutes. Add the turkey and cook until browned. Add the beans, tomatoes, chicken broth, and seasonings. Bring to a boil, then lower the heat and simmer, uncovered, for 30 minutes. You can serve this in individual hors d'oeuvre–size ramekins; or, depending on how your crowd rolls, put the pot on the table and give everyone a spoon.

ROMEO'S LOAVES AT FIRST SIGHT

You've tried it all: eHarmony, Match, Zoosk. You even checked out the other feline owners on Purrsonals.com. But don't give up! Like Christopher Marlowe wrote, and *As You Like It*'s Phoebe repeats: "Who ever loved that loved not at first sight?" You never know when you'll meet that special someone. Like Ferdinand and Miranda, when they have their "meet-cute after shipwreck" moment in *The Tempest*. Or Romeo when he first lays eyes on Juliet and realizes that his ex-girlfriend, Rosaline, was just a fling: "Did my heart love till now?" Why not host a cocktail party where everyone brings a single friend? You just might get struck by that same thunderbolt. So bake these loaves, and get ready to find the perfect match: maybe it's Brie, or prosciutto, or that cute guy in Apartment 4C. Because Love is as open as your choice of toppings. (But you might want to skip the garlic.) • *50–60 hors d'oeuvres*

> 1 teaspoon yeast
> 2½ teaspoons salt
> 1½ cups warm water, plus 1 tablespoon
> 3½ cups flour, plus extra for dusting
> Olive oil
> 1 egg white

In a mixing bowl, dissolve the yeast and salt in warm water. Add the flour slowly and mix thoroughly. On a surface dusted with flour, knead the dough and form it into a smooth ball. Grease another bowl with olive oil and place the dough inside. Turn the dough to cover evenly with oil. Cover with a dishcloth and let rise for 1 hour. Punch down and divide the dough into two equal parts. On a floured surface, roll and stretch the two halves into two 2-inch-wide logs, approximately 16 inches in length. Place the two loaves (with generous space between them) on an oiled cookie sheet. Cover and let rise for 30 minutes. While the dough is rising, preheat the oven to 400°F. When the dough is done rising, combine the egg white and remaining 1 tablespoon water in small bowl and brush the loaves with mixture. Bake for 40 minutes. Remove from the oven, cool, and cut thinly.

ANTONIO'S POUND OF MEATBALLS

It's easy to end up on the wrong side of the law when your best buddy is a mooch who's frittered away his trust fund. *The Merchant of Venice*'s Antonio suffers this fate when his profligate friend Bassanio asks him for yet more money—this time to impress the rich, eligible Portia. Antonio just can't say no. In fact, he's ready to give "My purse, my person, my extremest means" to make his friend's dreams come true. And this guy's not kidding when he says "extremest means." He goes to the money-lender Shylock to get the funds and agrees to put up a pound of his own flesh as collateral. Bassanio gets the girl, but Antonio gets arrested after he's unable to repay the loan. Then he faces certain death when Shylock insists on surgically extracting his payment. Luckily, a legal loophole prohibiting any bloodshed stops the operation and sets him free. He arrives at Bassanio and Portia's house ready to celebrate, but the new couple is ready to move on and leave the whole "unhappy subject" (aka Antonio) behind. Which means no "welcome back" cakes, no ale, no nothing. We've made this pound of bite-size meatballs for the party we wish *someone* had thrown for him. Whether you're welcoming your loved one back from college, prison, or rehab, they're the perfect addition to any homecoming. • *24 meatballs*

Olive oil spray
1 pound ground beef
¾ cup panko bread crumbs
1 egg
4 cloves garlic, peeled and crushed
2 tablespoons minced fresh thyme
2 tablespoons minced fresh tarragon
1 teaspoon salt
Pinch of pepper
¾ cup fig jam
2 tablespoons ketchup
3½ tablespoons chili sauce

Preheat the oven to 400°F and oil a baking sheet. Combine the meat, bread crumbs, egg, garlic, herbs, salt, and pepper in a mixing bowl. Mix thoroughly with your hands. Roll the mixture into tablespoon-size meatballs and place on the baking sheet. Bake for 15 minutes. While the meatballs are baking, prepare the sauce. Combine the jam, ketchup, and chili sauce in a saucepan. Cook on medium heat, stirring frequently, until the jam has dissolved. Combine the sauce and meatballs in a large, shallow bowl and serve with toothpicks.

THE MOTLEY FUL

There's no better occasion than an office party to really let loose and share all those opinions you've kept bottled up from nine to five. After three trips to the punch bowl, you're feeling the spirit of Shakespeare's candid and witty Fools who love to give their higher-ups the straight dope. Like when King Lear's Fool ribs him for letting his bossy daughters wear the pants in the family. Or when *As You Like It*'s Touchstone (the original "motley fool") tells Rosalind that her boyfriend's love poems are hackneyed drivel and asks: "Why do you infect yourself with them?" *She* could handle the truth, so why shouldn't your supervisor be able to when you give her some tough love about her new nose job? Not everyone will be your fan come Monday morning, but they're sure to keep coming back for more of *this* ful. • *2 cups*

1 medium onion, chopped

2 large tomatoes, seeded and chopped

3 tablespoons olive oil

1 (19-ounce) can fava beans, drained

3 cloves garlic, peeled and crushed

1 teaspoon ground cumin

1 teaspoon ground coriander

3 tablespoons fresh lemon juice

¼ teaspoon salt

¼ teaspoon pepper

¼ cup chopped cilantro

Lemon slice

Pita bread, cut into small triangles and toasted

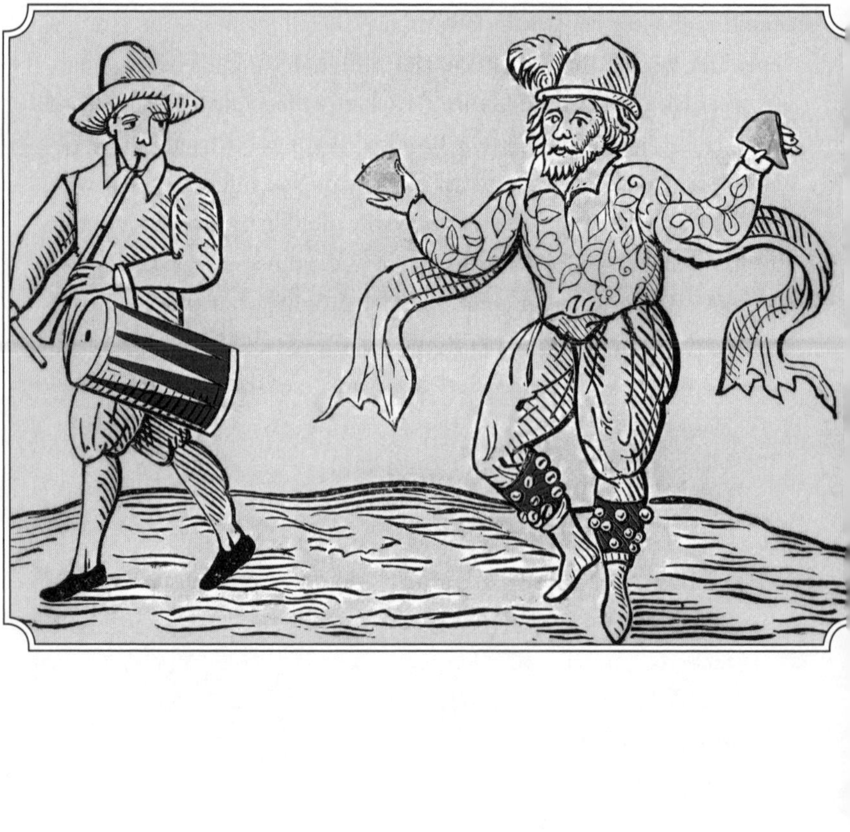

Shakespeare's Witty Fool was a later, more sophisticated version of the clownish comic-relief character. These earlier buffoons were played by fellow company member Will Kempe, who likely acted in the roles of Falstaff, Dogberry from *Much Ado About Nothing*, and Bottom in *A Midsummer Night's Dream*. Kempe was also famous for his dancing at a time when it was in vogue to end plays (even tragedies) with jigs. This talent eventually took Kempe away from Shakespeare's troupe around 1600, when he tried to pull a Justin Timberlake by going out on his own. His debut solo act was a one-hundred-mile jig from London to Norwich, which he chronicled in *Kemp's Nine Days' Wonder . . . Written by Himself to Satisfy His Friends*. His departure, and the arrival of his replacement, the more sophisticated comic Robert Armin, likely contributed to Shakespeare's development of the clever Fool character in his later plays—like Touchstone and King Lear's wise-cracking companion.

Sauté the onion and tomatoes in oil on medium heat, until the onion starts to become translucent. Turn down the heat to medium-low and add the fava beans and garlic. Cook for 15 minutes, stirring frequently. Stir in the cumin, coriander, lemon juice, salt, and pepper. Transfer the mixture to a food processor and puree. Serve topped with the cilantro and lemon slice, accompanied by toasted pita triangles.

FALSTAFF'S PAUNCH SLIDERS

Falstaff is the original one-man party animal. That "fat rogue" consumes all things with gusto—women, food, and drink—and wears his supersize love of life proudly. Whether he's drinking with Prince Hal in

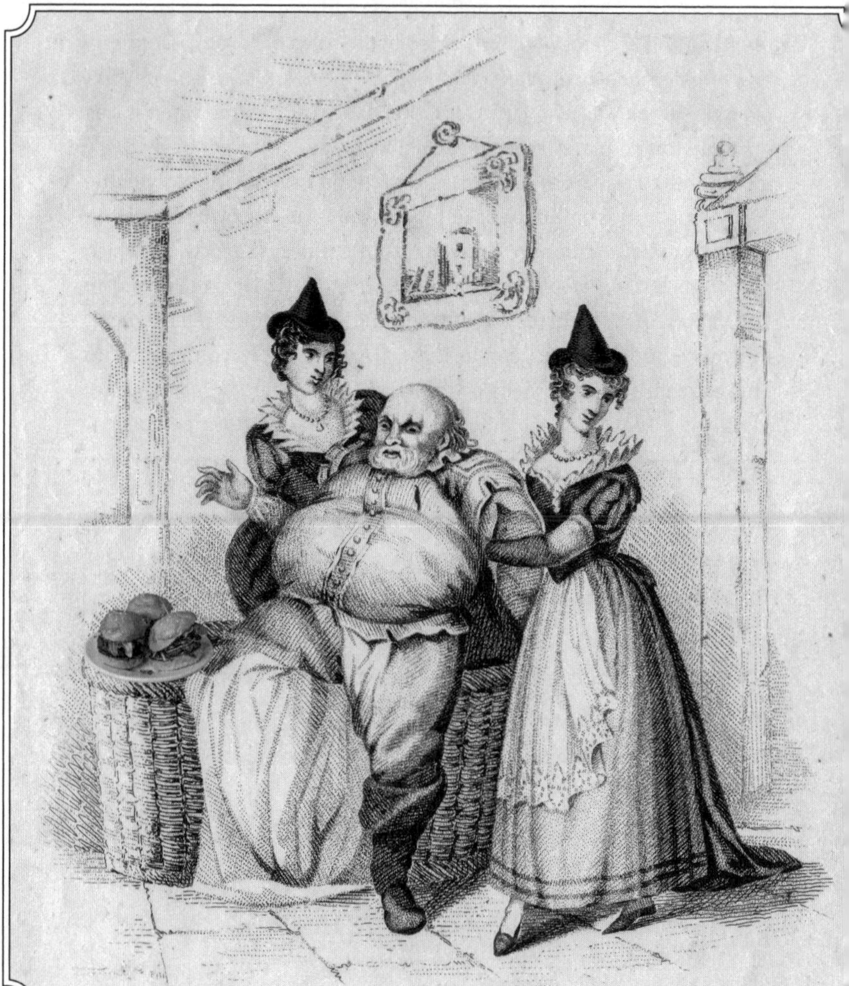

the history plays, or wooing "both high and low, both rich and poor" in the comedy *The Merry Wives of Windsor*, this guy can have fun anywhere with anyone in any genre. So when you want to get a party started but don't have any particular occasion to celebrate, pull a Falstaff: invite over everyone you've ever met and have a huge bash just for the hell of it! Have your guests bring a six-pack, and fry up a pile of these paunch sliders. Or, better yet, tell your guests to do it while you drink their beer. • *24 hors d'oeuvres*

TOMATO AND STRAWBERRY RELISH

5 Roma tomatoes, skins and seeds removed, then chopped

8 large strawberries, chopped

1 teaspoon sugar

½ teaspoon balsamic vinegar

¼ cup fresh mint, finely chopped

1 pound ground lamb

2 tablespoons madeira wine

1 tablespoon fresh lemon juice

1 clove garlic, peeled and crushed

½ cup chopped arugula

1 medium onion, finely chopped

½ teaspoon cumin

½ teaspoon coriander

1 tablespoon Dijon mustard

Salt and pepper

3 tablespoons olive oil

Slider buns; or mini brioche buns, quartered

In a saucepan, prepare the relish by cooking the tomatoes, strawberries, and sugar on medium-high heat for 15 minutes. Reduce to medium and cook for another 10 minutes. Remove from heat and stir in the balsamic vinegar and mint. Set aside.

In a bowl, mix together the lamb, wine, lemon juice, garlic, arugula, onion, cumin, coriander, mustard, salt and pepper to taste, and 1 tablespoon oil. Form into patties, 1 inch in diameter. In a large skillet, heat the remaining 2 tablespoons oil over high heat. Brown the sliders for approximately 2 minutes on each side, turning once. Press the sliders down when turning. Let cool to room temperature. Top the sliders with a spoonful of relish and place on buns or between two brioche wedges. Secure with festive toothpicks. Indulge.

IMAGE CREDITS

page viii   Gebbie & Co., *Mrs. D. P. Bowers as Lady Macbeth*. Photogravure, circa 1887. Folger Shakespeare Library, Art File B786, no. 2.

page xiv   Francis Legat, *Hamlet, act IV, scene V*. Based on a painting by Benjamin West. Engraving, 1802. Folger Shakespeare Library, Art File S528h1, no. 160.

page 2   Matt Stretch, *Mr. Barry Sullivan as Richard III*. Drawing, 1876. Folger Shakespeare Library, Art Box S915, no. 3.

page 6   *Miss Glyn and Mr. Hoskins as Isabella and Lucio in "Measure for Measure."* Engraving from a daguerreotype by Paine of Islington, nineteenth century. Folger Shakespeare Library, Art File G568, no. 2.

page 10   J. Duncombe, *Edgar and the Duke of Gloster Meeting King Lear*. Print, early nineteenth century. Folger Shakespeare Library, Art File S528k6, no. 35.

page 18   Felix Octavius Carr Darley, *Macbeth, Act II, scene II*. Drawing, 1886. Folger Shakespeare Library, Art Box D221, no. 47.

page 22   Ralph Gardiner, page 110 of *England's Grievance Discovered*. 1655. Folger Shakespeare Library, 139–623q.

page 28   A. M. Faulkner, *Antony and Cleopatra*. Drawing, 1906. Folger Shakespeare Library, Art Box F263, no. 1.

page 31   Louis Rhead, *Softly Unloosing the Bracelet from Her Arm*. Drawing, 1918. Folger Shakespeare Library, Art Box R469, no. 54.

page 34   Robert Anning Bell, *The Masque of the Graceful Dance*. Drawing, 1901. Folger Shakespeare Library, Art Box B433, no. 10.

page 37   J. E. Pawsey, *As You Like It, act II, scene IV*. Drawing, 1898. Folger Shakespeare Library, Art Box P339, no. 1.

page 39   *Miss Fanny Kemble as Juliet.* Engraving, mid-nineteenth century. Folger Shakespeare Library, Art File K31.3, no. 12.

page 46   Louis Rhead, *"A Midsummer Night's Dream," Puck on a Mushroom.* Drawing, 1918. Folger Shakespeare Library, Art Box R469, no. 106.

page 50   William Francis Sterling, *Henry IV (first part), act III, scene IV.* Engraving, nineteenth century. Folger Shakespeare Library, Art File S528k1a, no. 31.

page 54   Cornelis Metsys, *Henricus dei gra[tia] rex Anglie.* Engraving, 1548. Folger Shakespeare Library, Art 252711.

page 58   Solomon Alexander Hart, *Othello and Iago.* Engraving, mid- to late-nineteenth century. Folger Shakespeare Library, Art File S52801, no. 26.

page 60   *R. B. Mantell as Macbeth.* Photograph, late nineteenth century/early twentieth century. Folger Shakespeare Library, Art File M292.8, no. 5.

page 68   Benjamin J. Falk, *Edward Harrigan and Annie Yeamans in Unidentified Roles.* Photograph, late nineteenth/early twentieth century. Folger Shakespeare Library, Art File H297, no. 1.

page 71   *Rosalind and Celia.* In *Plays . . . from the Corrected Text of Johnson and Steevens.* Plate, 1807. Folger Shakespeare Library, PR2752 1807c, copy 4, vol. 7.

page 73   Louis Rhead, *Helena Pursues Demetrius.* Engraving, 1918. Folger Shakespeare Library, Art Box R469, no. 79.

page 77   Richard Rhodes, *A Midsummer Night's Dream, act III, scene I, Titania.* Engraving from painting by Henry Fuseli, late eighteenth/early nineteenth century. Folger Shakespeare Library, Art File S528m5, no. 40.

page 82   Samuel Rowlands, *Tis Merrie When Gossips Meete.* Title page, 1613. Folger Shakespeare Library, STC 21410.2.

page 85   *The Attitudes of Miss Fanny Kemble as Juliet.* Lithograph, late nineteenth century, after 1829 engraving. Folger Shakespeare Library, Art File K31.3, no. 6.

page 87   William Camden, *Annales: The True and Royall History of the Famous Empresse Elizabeth Queene of England France and Ireland.* Frontispiece portrait, 1625. Folger Shakespeare Library, STC 4497, copy 1.

page 94 J. Coghlan, *Troilus and Cressida, act IV, scene II*. Watercolor, early nineteenth century. Folger Shakespeare Library, Art Box C678, no. 16.

page 96 Thomas Bragg, *The Winter's Tale, Antigonus*. Engraving, 1807. Folger Shakespeare Library, Art File S528w1, no. 22.

page 99 William G. Jackman, *Ophelia*. Engraving, nineteenth century. Folger Shakespeare Library, Art File S528h1, no. 84.

page 104 Jacob Tonson, *Pericles, act III, scene II*. Engraving, 1709. Folger Shakespeare Library, Art File S528p1, no. 5.

page 108 James Roberts, *Mr. Yates in the Character of Malvolio*. Engraving, 1776. Folger Shakespeare Library, Art File Y34, no. 2.

page 112 Robert Anning Bell, *The Masque of Courteous Monsters*. Drawing, 1901. Folger Shakespeare Library, Art Box B433, no. 49.

page 115 Robert Anning Bell, frontispiece to Act I of Bell's edition of *The Tempest*. Drawing, 1901. Folger Shakespeare Library, Art Box B433, no. 56.

page 117 Louis Rhead, *Macbeth, act IV, scene I*. Drawing, 1918. Folger Shakespeare Library, Art Box R469, no. 86.

page 120 Gebbie & Co., *Edwin Forrest as King Lear*. Photogravure, circa 1887. Folger Shakespeare Library, Art File F728, no. 13.

page 122 J. Duncombe, *Death of Cleopatra, Queen of Egypt from the Poisonous Bite of an Asp*. Print, early nineteenth century. Folger Shakespeare Library, Art File S528a3, no. 32.

page 134 William Kemp, fl. 1600, *Kemps Nine Daies Wonder Performed in a Daunce from London to Norwich*. With an introduction and notes by Rev. Alexander Dyce. Title page, 1840. Folger Shakespeare Library, PN2598. K6 1839.

page 136 George Adcock, *The Merry Wives of Windsor, act III, scene III*. Engraving, early to mid-nineteenth century. Folger Shakespeare Library, Art File S528m4, no. 51.

ACKNOWLEDGMENTS

If it weren't for our super-agents, Adriann Ranta and Allison Devereux at Wolf Literary Services, we'd still be sitting at a bar punning to ourselves. Thank you for picking us out of the slush pile, cleaning us up, and making us presentable. You answered every question and solved every problem. Thank you to Meg Leder at Penguin for believing in our writing and in this book; and to our editor at Perigee, Jeanette Shaw, and art director, Tiffany Estreicher, for expertly guiding it to completion. Jim Monaco was the mastermind behind the book's images. Thank you for figuring out how to turn a bear into a beer, and an eyeball into an hors d'oeuvre. At the Folger Shakespeare Library, Garland Scott supported this project from the start; and Julie Ainsworth helped us navigate the library's rich collection of digital images.

We're grateful to our friends in the writing business, who were always at the ready with professional advice and support: Adam Barr, Amy Boesky, Beth Frankl, Melissa Hinebauch, Marjorie Ingall, Donna Friedman Meir, Christopher Monks, John Norman (who got our blog up and running), Adam Peck, Mary Beth Pemberton, John Plotz, John Ross, Leslie Silbert, and Patricia Wen.

Our recipes wouldn't be as delicious without the many friends who helped us test and create them: Mark Barer, Pontus Berghe, Jenny Dahlstein, Maggie Dey, Ellen Geller, Lucy Goodhart, Mugi Hanao, Heeten Kalan, Benna Kushlefsky, Noa and Zvika Neeman, Charlie Radin, Liz Reynolds, Laura Rysman, Max Senter, and Shanna Shulman. And a special shout-out to Winestone's Patrick Dubsky and Teresa Murray for teaching us how to layer Irish cream, finding us wormwood bitters, and letting us do shots in their store.

We are indebted to Heather Dubrow, Roland Greene, Judith Haber, Stephen Orgel, Patricia Parker, Heyden White Rostow, and Susanne Wofford for teaching us how to read and love Shakespeare. And for keeping the Bard love alive in Boston, warm thanks to William Carroll, Mary Crane, Coppélia Kahn, Diana Henderson, and Linda McJannet.

A big thank-you to all our department colleagues who make us think *and* laugh. And to our students at Boston College, Worcester Polytechnic Institute, and the Bread Loaf School of English for keeping it real.

For their unconditional love and support, our deepest gratitude goes to Michele Baker, David, Marian, John, Jenny, and Ned Bicks, Alanya Bostwick, Alison Dagnes, Ruth and Frank Ephraim, Dana Gershon, Lauren Glickman, Marin Hagen, Rachel Hamilton, Eleanne Hattis, Laura Hitchcock, Linda Kahn, Jim Morgan, Fiona Murray, the Reay family, Gladys and Alex Rysman and the entire Rysman clan, Andrea Kaston Tange, and Grace Won.

And finally, to our husbands, Brendon Reay and Marc Rysman; our kids, Annabel, Jonah, Ava, Micah, and Amalia; and our dogs, Hank and Chuck. Thank you for giving us lots of material to work with. And so many reasons to celebrate.

INDEX

Page numbers in *italics* indicate illustrations; those followed by "n" indicate notes.

ABOUT THE AUTHORS

Caroline Bicks is associate professor of English at Boston College and is also on the faculty of the Bread Loaf School of English. She specializes in Shakespeare, gender studies, and the history of science. Her book, *Midwiving Subjects in Shakespeare's England*, will make you grateful to be living in a world with epidurals. Her creative nonfiction has appeared on NPR, in the "Modern Love" column of the *New York Times*, and in the show and book *Afterbirth: Stories You Won't Read in a Parenting Magazine*. She and Michelle have blogged at *Everyday Shakespeare* for years, and together they've written Bard Meets Life humor for *McSweeney's Internet Tendency* and *Errant Parent*. She loves a good drink, a good laugh, her husband, and their two kids. Not necessarily in that order.

Michelle Ephraim is associate professor of English at Worcester Polytechnic Institute, where she teaches courses on Shakespeare, early modern drama, and creative writing. She's the author of the book *Reading the Jewish Woman on the Elizabethan Stage* and articles on adultery, religious conversion, and other controversial matters in Shakespeare's plays. Most recently, she's written about Shakespeare in North American popular culture and the comic series *Kill Shakespeare*. Her personal essays and humor pieces have appeared in *Tikkun*, *Lilith*, *The Morning News*, *Word Riot*, and the *Washington Post*. She lives in Boston with her husband and three children. She'll tell you more over a cocktail and some salty snacks.